Eric Gill
Work is sacred

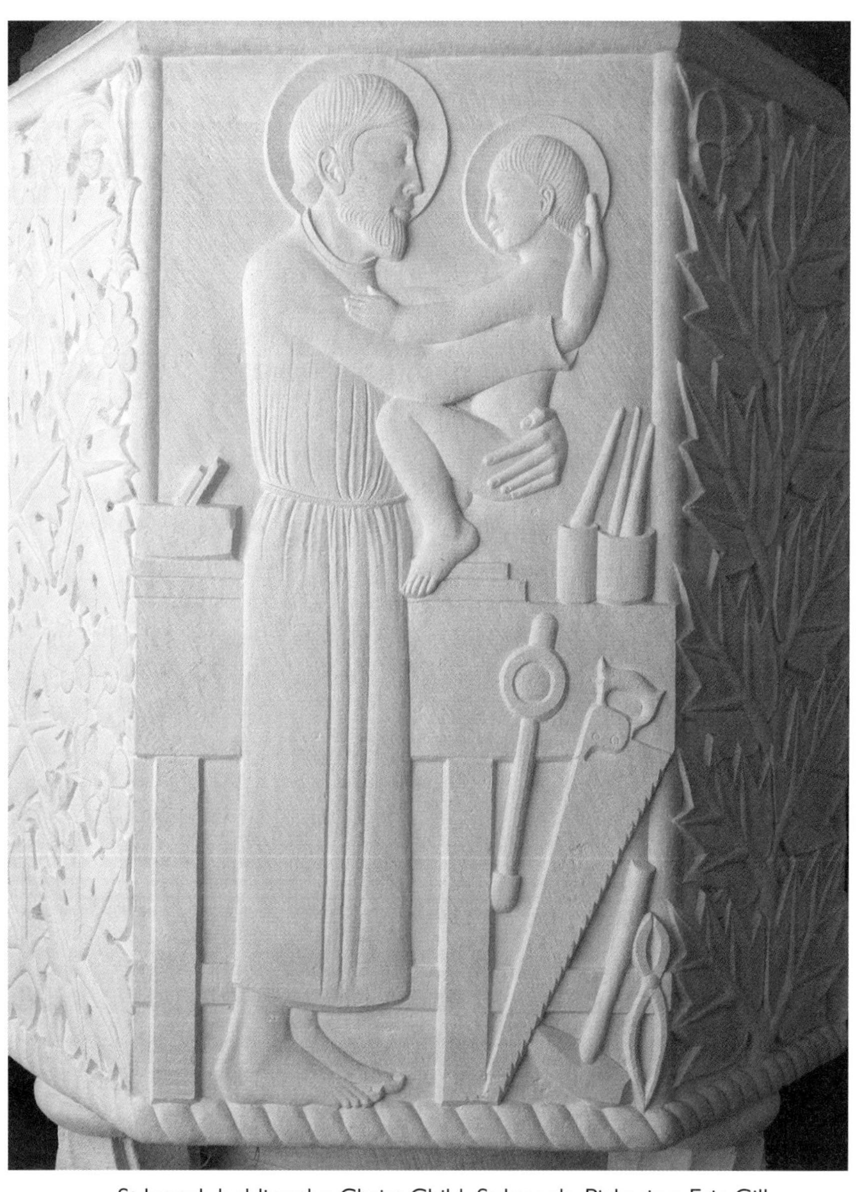

St Joseph holding the Christ Child, St Joseph, Pickering. Eric Gill.

Eric Gill
Work is Sacred

edited by
Martin John Broadley

Catholic Archives Society

Published by Catholic Archives Society
The Editor, 88A Manchester Road, Worsley
Manchester M28 3LN

British Library Cataloguing-in-Publication Data
A catalogue record for this book is available from the British Library

First published 2013

ISBN   978 0 86088 046 2

Typeset in Perpetua with Gill Sans
by Koinonia, Manchester
Printed in Great Britain
by Bell & Bain Ltd, Glasgow

Contents

List of plates and figures

List of plates

1 *Madonna* by Eric Gill, painted by Desmond Chute c.1919. Reproduced from the Eric Gill Collection at the West Sussex Record Office by permission of the County Archivist.

2 Hampshire House Workshop. Wood engraving, 1915. Reproduced from the originals held by the Department of Special Collections of the University Libraries of Notre Dame.

3 Doves Bakery. St Dominic's Press. Wood engraving, 1916. Reproduced from the originals held by the Department of Special Collections of the University Libraries of Notre Dame

4 St Dominic's Press, includes Eric Gill's engraving of the hound of St. Dominic, 1923. Reproduced from the originals held by the Department of Special Collections of the University Libraries of Notre Dame.

5 *Fifth Station of the Cross.* Gill's second drawing for a trial panel to be submitted to the Westminster Cathedral authorities for approval. Reproduced by kind permission of Manchester City Art Gallery.

6 Eric Gill's watercolour sketch of St Peter's, Gorleston. Reproduced by kind permission of the William Andrews Clark Memorial Library, UCLA.

List of figures

Front cover, Eric Gill in his workroom at Capel-y-ffin. Reproduced from the originals held by the Department of Special Collections of the University Libraries of Notre Dame.

Frontispiece, St Joseph holding the Christ Child, St Joseph, Pickering. Eric Gill. Reproduced by kind permission of the Patrimony Committee of the Bishops' Conference of England and Wales. Photograph by Alex Ramsey.

1 *East* [*recte* West] *Pallant*, Chichester. Eric Gill, 1900. Reproduced from the Eric Gill Collection at the West Sussex Record Office by permission of the County Archivist.

The Figures are placed between pages 30–31 and 74–75.

Acknowledgements

I would like to acknowledge the help and support received during the preparation and final stages of this centenary anthology. First and foremost, thanks must go to officers and members of the council of the Catholic Archives Society of Great Britain and the Republic of Ireland for their suggestion and encouragement that the work presented here be published, and for providing the means to make this possible. Special thanks must of course be given to all the contributors. To Ruth Cribb and Naomi Billingsley for their recommendations regarding content, and to Dorothy Clayton, John Hodgson, Stella Halkyard, Christine Hill for reading the manuscript at various stages and kindly offering suggestions and making corrections. Emma Marigliano of the Portico Library, Manchester, contributed valuable ideas, and not least very much hard work and time, toward the layout and presentation. Numerous individuals, and members of staff from galleries and libraries both in England and America provided a very kind and efficient service in supplying images and granting permission for their reproduction: Sophie Andreae of the Patrimony Committee of the Catholic Bishops' Conference; Tracy Bergstrom, University of Notre Dame; Adrian Brink, James Clarke & Co; the County Archivist and staff at the West Sussex Record Office; Louisa Dare, Courtauld Gallery, London; Joe Cribb; Br Michael Curran FSC; Andrew Derrick; Ditchling Museum of Art+Craft; Scott Jacobs, Clark Library, UCLA; Fr Fergus Kerr OP; Louise North, BBC Written Archives; John Sherman, University of Notre Dame; Tracy Walker, Manchester City Art Gallery; library staff at the Tate Gallery, London; Sara Weber, Dept of Rare Books & Special Collections, University of Notre Dame. Finally, special words of thanks are owed to Dolor MacCarron who read the final draft, any errors remaining are mine.

Martin John Broadley
Editor

Introduction

M. J. Broadley

The centenary of Eric Gill's birth was marked by Malcolm Yorke's aptly titled, *Eric Gill Man of Flesh and Spirit* (London, 1981). The purpose of that study was to enable 'a new generation of artists and readers to encounter [Gill's] ideas and work.'[1] Although choosing to omit Gill's Catholic theological writings, Yorke acknowledged his conversion to Catholicism as 'simply the most important event in his life, and his claim in the *Autobiography* that all the other happenings after that were mere postscripts is not an affectation.'[2] Yorke identifies two 'great moving forces' in Gill's life; one was religion, the other was his sexuality.[3] Since those observations were made the extent and problematic nature of Gill's sexual compulsions have become publicly known. Fiona MacCarthy's biography of Gill[4] reveals the shocking and at times sordid details of the sexual practices recorded by Gill in his diaries, evidencing a disturbing anomaly in his life. In the light of her findings MacCarthy writes: '[A]t least I can be confident that Gill was not what he said he was.'[5] Fr Brocard Sewell, who was acquainted with Gill, wrote of how 'most people who knew him – and these included his parish priest – considered him a holy man. This idea is now, since the disclosures concerning his sexual antinomianism in Fiona MacCarthy's new biography, less easy to maintain.'[6]

This anthology, in acknowledging the centenary of Gill's conversion to Catholicism, seeks to view him from the context of the first of those 'great moving forces'. The chapters which follow explore the significance of Gill's faith and how it influenced and fashioned his work and thought. Catholicism

1 Malcolm Yorke, *Eric Gill Man of Flesh and Spirit* (London, 1981), p. 19.

2 *Ibid.*, p. 41.

3 *Ibid.*, p. 41.

4 Fiona MacCarthy, *Eric Gill* (London, 1989).

5 *Ibid.*, p. x.

6 Eric Gill, *Servile Labour and Contemplation. With a forward by Fr Brocard Sewell*, (The Aylesford Press, 1989), p. 14.

is centrally, one might say doubly, important for an understanding of Gill. First, from the point of view of his art, as noted by his brother Cecil:

> I don't suggest that one must be a Catholic to understand Eric's argument: indeed many Catholics are impervious to it, but the essence of his teaching is central to the Catholic faith and rightly to understand the one you must at least understand the other.[7]

Analysis of Gill's 'sexual antinomianism' lies beyond the scope of this present work; it rests with those who have the prerequisite theological and psychological knowledge to deal with such matters. Here again Catholicism's doctrine of sin, nature and grace is the perspective that potentially offers the most adequate approach to this sensitive issue. The Catholic tradition in moral theology, with its insights into the complexity of the human person, provides a lens through which to view the dichotomy inherent in fallen human nature.

The chapters follow chronologically the course of Gill's life; the corresponding developments in his ideas and significant commissions with which they deal act as milestones in the course of the narrative. Timothy J. McCann, former Assistant County Archivist at the West Sussex Record Office, writes of the life-long significance of Chichester in Gill's life as being a time of his awakening to lettering, love, beauty and form. The Eric Gill Collection at the West Sussex Record Office is home to an important collection of his drawings, sculptures and miscellaneous personal papers. John Skelton, Gill's nephew and last apprentice, described it as covering 'every facet of Gill's multifarious creative activities'. Chichester was deeply symbolic for Gill, representing 'the place where life and work and things were all in one and all in harmony'.[8] It became a source from where he drew ideas about life and society. There Gill would spend much time drawing locomotives; these make up a significant part of the Record Office's collection of his earlier drawings. This interest in locomotives dispels the misconception that he was naturally opposed to machines. At Chichester Gill made the important personal discovery of 'form', which he defined as 'the soul of a thing'. Equally formative experiences were his falling under the influence of his art master, George Herbert Catto, who represented 'the good and the true and the beautiful', and becoming friends with the Cathedral Prebendary, Dr Robert Henry Coddrington, whom Gill described as 'an angel of enlightenment'. Gill's friendship with Coddrington was an open sesame to the Cathedral and all its hidden places, and no doubt was effective in his transition from drawing engines to architecture. Gill always remained

---

7 BBC Written Archives, 'My Brother, Eric Gill', Dr Cecil Gill, 20 Mar. 1951. [BBC WA]

8 Eric Gill, *Autobiography* (London,), cited below, p. 6.

deeply moved by the Cathedral's reliefs of the Raising of Lazarus and Christ's arrival at the house of Mary and Martha. At Chichester he became enthralled with church music and services in the Cathedral. Here too, he became, as he described it, 'mad on lettering'; an experience which was to lead to a complete change in ambition. The third influential person he met at Chichester, and the most significant of all, was Ethel Mary Moore, his future wife. In correspondence regarding the repair or restoration of Chichester's Market Cross Gill enters the debate of the incongruity – and absurdity – of imagining that 'that 20th century workmen can, however skilful they are, transport themselves back into the 16th century'. This would prove to be one of many reoccurring themes. Integrity was to become a watchword; Gill could not understand why one should want to pretend to be a Gothic workman.

Joe Cribb, Coordinator of the Eric Gill Society, continues the story as we see Gill move from London to the Sussex village of Ditchling, and make the important spiritual journey of becoming a Catholic. Gill lived at Ditchling from 1907 to 1924. Correspondence at the newly-opened Ditchling Museum of Art + Craft provides important help to the researcher in gaining detail of Gill's progress as both artist and Catholic thinker. By calling attention to a key document in its archive Joe Cribb gives a valuable insight into Gill's conversion. This important piece of evidence is in fact a letter to Everard Meynell written by Gill in which he speaks of his rejection of Socialism and Fabianism, his disenchantment with the Arts and Crafts Movement, and his desire to seek instruction, with a view to being received into the Catholic Church. This was no sudden whim, but a logical development in his search for Truth. 1913 was a key year for Gill's development as an artist, for it was when he was given the commission to carve the Station of the Cross at Westminster Cathedral. His new found faith would influence his more intimate art work. This we see illustrated in Gill's wood engravings and carvings of the Crucifixion, illustrated in figures 3 & 4. Whilst at Ditchling the foundations of a community of craftsmen were laid, this would evolve into the Guild of St Joseph and St Dominic, whose members were Dominican tertiaries.[9] The figure of Fr Vincent McNabb OP, and other members of the Order of Preachers were highly influential in this venture. The startling image of 'The Nuptials of God' (fig. 6) caused McNabb much consternation (the image had originally been intended as an ordination for Fr Gerald Vann OP). For Gill it visualises the mystical union between Christ and the

---

9   James R. Lothian believes that, '[t]he community of craftsmen and artists that Gill established at Ditchling constituted his most significant contribution to the English Catholic intellectual community.' Cf. James R. Lothian, *The Making and Unmaking of the English Catholic Intellectual Community, 1910–1950* (Notre Dame, 2009), p. 89.

Church. Yorke notes how Gill, 'found much comfort in the Catholic Church's tolerance of the body, and its precept that "Man is composed of matter and spirit, both real and both good."'[10]

Professor John Sherman's chapter illustrates the field of work and the ideals espoused by Gill and the Guild of St Joseph and St Dominic. His contribution draws upon the University of Notre Dame's Gill Collection, with special reference to the posters printed by St Dominic's Press. The influence of the one-time craft community at Hammersmith, and the importance of the relationship between Gill and Hilary (Douglas) Pepler are also central features to this chapter, thus providing evidence of a wider sphere of influence upon Gill's development as artist and thinker. The posters reproduced below portray some of the issues with which Gill was concerned in his role as public speaker; for example, unemployment, the detrimental effect of machines, and Distributism. The latter was based on the encyclicals *Rerum Novarum* and *Quadragesimo Anno*; Gill's version of Distributism was particularly vigorous.[11] The influence of the Dominicans once again comes to the fore: in the figures of such people as Fr Hugh Pope, Fr Hilary Carpenter, and of course Fr Vincent McNabb.

Sculptures of the Crucifixion constitute the largest category in Gill's output. Naomi Billingsley in her chapter 'Conversion by Commission' explores the significance of Gill's first major commission as a Catholic – the Stations of the Cross at Westminster Cathedral. This commission was crucial to the development in his ideas of Art and Beauty. They also represent an important chapter in the history of the Cathedral itself. In an article written post-completion of the Westminster Stations, and using the pseudonym "Rowton", Gill stated how the artist is not the creator of Beauty but rather its servant.[12] Judith Collins has written of how Gill 'knew that he was making his work to please God',[13] this idea comes out strongly in the case of the Westminster commission. As does the influence of Thomistic theology; which Gill gleaned from, among other sources, his reading of Jacques Maritain's *Art et Scholastique*. Naomi Billingsley demonstrates Gill's indebtedness to the scholastic tradition prior to reading Maritain. This chapter, and that of Br Michael Curran FSC (*Chapter Seven*), enable one to see a development in Gill's thinking and the way he portrayed his thoughts. Whilst the Westminster series are neutral, a later series carved in wood – the subject of Br Michael's chapter – portray his views on social justice.

---

10   Yorke, *op. cit.*, p. 18.

11   Lothian, notes how Gill's 'interpretation of Distributism proved too radical even for many Bellocians' [followers of Belloc's economic theories]. *op. cit.*, p. 107.

12   See below, pp. 37ff.

13   Judith Collins, *Eric Gill the Sculpture* (London, 1998), p. 11.

During a 1949 radio broadcast entitled 'My Brother, Eric Gill', Cecil Gill referred to a letter he received from his elder sibling on the occasion when he too had become a Catholic. Eric Gill wrote: 'For the theologians agree; there is no valid distinction between the sacred and the profane.'[14] The question of the sacred and the secular remained a central theme throughout Gill's life, both in his thought and art. Ruth Cribb's chapter on his public sculpture, namely the BBC sculptures of 'Prospero and Ariel', concentrates on how he applied this important concept in this particular, and highly significant, commission. It also raises important issues regarding the complexities of Gill's character *vis-à-vis* his patrons and clients. In, 'Eric Gill in Manchester' attention moves from consideration of his visual art to an examination of Gill's thoughts on finance, morality and social justice. The lecture entitled 'Money and Morals' which Gill gave in Manchester in 1933 has been seen as a watershed in his political and philosophical ideas, and so is a further milestone marking the passage of his life. The later Gill is seen in the two final chapters. Brother Michael Curran FSC, not only reveals the history behind the recently re-discovered wooden Stations of the Cross – which remained unaccounted for when Judith Collins was writing her catalogue raisonné – but also demonstrates how these represent a significant advancement in Gill's understanding of and approach to the subject. Finally, Andrew Derrick's treatment of 'an unexpected late flowering' of Gill's talents – his design of the church of St Peter the Apostle, Gorleston-on-Sea – concludes the anthology appropriately with what has been described as the 'summation of [Gill's] work and beliefs.'[15] This is encapsulated in the question which Gill endeavoured to address with regard to the Gorleston project: what is a church? The answer to this question – like those corresponding to questions about money and morals – stems from a critique of the capitalist system. The solution he proposed was typically revolutionary: the altar must be placed in the centre of the church, surrounded by the people, in order to facilitate greater participation by the people.

What follows are in many ways but glimpses into areas of Gill's work and thought, some of which warrant greater and more detailed study. Several of the contributors have used hitherto unknown or unexplored sources; recent events have made archive material and primary sources relating to Gill and his circle of like-minded craftsmen more readily and easily available. The recent re-opening of the Ditchling Museum of Art + Craft, the depositing of the archives of the English Dominican Province at Douai Abbey Library, and the cataloguing of the Gill Archive at Westminster Cathedral will greatly facilitate such research.

14   BBC WA, 'My Brother, Eric Gill' Dr Cecil Gill, 20 Mar. 1951.
15   Cf. p. 82 below.

The Eric Gill Collection at Chichester

Timothy J. McCann

The West Sussex Record Office at Chichester holds an important collection of material relating to Eric Gill, which includes books, drawings, engravings, sculptures and a significant quantity of miscellaneous personal papers. The collection was formed there because Eric Gill is associated with Chichester, having lived there for a time and because the city played a part in his art, in his life and in his writings.

In his *Autobiography* Gill wrote that he 'left school in 1897, primarily, I suppose, because the family moved to Chichester'. He went on to describe the overwhelming impression the city had made on him when he first visited:

> One day in the summer of 1897, while my father was still a student at the Theological College, I bicycled over from Brighton to see him. I have only an intangible recollection of that day but it is not the mere haziness of memory which prevents me from describing it. Nor is it that the vision is not clear and, in some particulars, even precise. It is simply that the thing is beyond words. You must understand that except for that one day I had never, in all my fifteen years, seen anything like it.
>
> It had simply never occurred to me before that day that towns could have a shape and be, like my beloved locomotives, things with character and meaning. If you had been drawing 'engines' for years and were then suddenly taken to such a city, you would instantly see what I mean. I had not been training myself to become an engineer, I had been training myself to see Chichester, the human-city, the city of God, the place where life and work and things were all in one and all in harmony. That, without words, was how it seemed to me that day. It was not its picturesqueness; for Chichester is the least picturesque of cathedral cities. It wasn't its antiquity; for I had learned no history and age meant little to me. It was a town, a city, a thing planned and ordered – no mere congeries of more or less sordid streets, growing, like a fungus wherever the network of railways and sidings and railway sheds would allow. That, I discovered, was mainly what Brighton was to me ... I only knew that Chichester was what Brighton was not, an end, a thing, a place, the product of reason and love. For love too was visible. Here was no dead product of mathematical calculation, no merely sanitary and

convenient arrangement. Here was something as human as home and as lovely as heaven. That was how it seemed to me, and I went back to Brighton on my bicycle in the evening in a glow of excitement.[1]

Gill had left school when the family moved from Brighton, but he did not immediately settle to training for a career. Instead he took advantage of what the city had to offer him. He wrote:

> Now began a new life, a miraculous life, a life as it were in fairyland. I think it may not be difficult for the reader to understand this. Anyone who has lived for the first ten or fifteen years of childhood in such a place as suburban Brighton and has then, almost suddenly been taken, with all the natural enthusiasm of childhood for green fields and pastures new, to live in such a truly noble town as Chichester will understand; and I think even those who have not had such an experience will see that the contrast must have been almost frightening in its violence. For even if a Brighton suburb is not more than usually shapeless, not more shapeless than all such nineteenth-century towns are and must naturally be – for they are the product of nothing nobler than the speculative builder's appetite for money – on the other hand the 'ancient and loyal' city of Chichester is more than usually serene and orderly. And it owes its quality not merely to the civil and religious exuberance of the medieval world but, more fundamentally, to the military and civic order of Rome. The small modern growth of the town outside the walls was, forty years ago, almost negligible. Over more than half the length of the Roman wall (a great part of which is thick enough to form a broad footpath along the top) you could look straight out into the green fields. A town, a city, of ten thousand persons, with the Cathedral, the Bishop's and canons' houses, ten parish churches and twice as many 'public' houses – four straight, wide main streets dividing the city into nearly equal quarters and the residential south-eastern quarter similarly again divided by four small streets and these almost completely filled with seventeenth- and eighteenth-century houses.[2]

Gill mentioned that 'from my earliest years I had always been fond of drawing engines and bridges and signals and tunnels. As time went on this enthusiasm was canalised more and more into the drawing of locomotives.'[3] There exists a common misconception that Gill was opposed to machines. The scrap books that he kept while he first lived in Chichester are overflowing with pictures of engines, machines, and locomotives and many of his earlier drawings in the Record Office collection are of locomotives or railway machinery. But he soon expanded his range of interests under the influence of his surroundings:

1   Eric Gill, *Autobiography* (London, 1944), pp. 75–6.
2   *Ibid.*, pp. 78–81.
3   *Ibid.*, p. 73.

I had just come from a period of intense concentration upon the particular form of a particular thing. For now I will use the word 'form' rather than the word 'shape'. Form, though of course I didn't know it for many years later, is a much bigger word than shape. Shape is only the visible aspect of form. The soul of a thing is its form. And though I knew nothing about it, and no one ever talked to me in such terms – though – perhaps, nay, certainly, the hard core of my father's sentimentality was that very thing, even if he didn't know it himself – that was, in fact, the thing I had really been concerned with during all those years of 'engine' drawing.[4]

Among his Chichester drawings are two of Tower Street in 1900; two of West Pallant in 1900 (Fig. 1); one of Canon Gate in 1900; one of the Cathedral from Pallant House in 1900 and a later one of the doorway of John Edes House in West Street. Indeed, it was with doorways that Gill first came to public notice. In 1900 he won a prize for his watercolour sketches of Chichester doorways in a national competition and made his first appearance in print in the December issue of *The Building News*. The short article, entitled, 'Chichester Doorways', reproduced these nine watercolours and Gill's description of them, which lacks something of the elegance of style he achieved by the time he wrote his *Autobiography*, and illustrates his slightly uncertain grasp of the city's history, though it must be remembered that he was only eighteen at the time.

Distance does seem to lend enchantment. Gill is noticeably less enthusiastic about the city as an eighteen-year-old than when remembering his youth from the sanctuary of Capel-y-fin. Some sixty years later, Francis Steer developed Gill's ideas in his charming *A Selection of Chichester Doorways. Chichester Papers, no.18*. 'And what I had put into drawing locomotives, I now put into drawing churches, and doorways and towers', Gill continued in his *Autobiography*:

> …and with this advantage: that now I was, for a time, released from any consideration of earning a living. When I drew locomotives people said: Oh, you're going to be an engineer; you'll 'get on', you'll make money. But when they saw me drawing churches, they didn't worry me like that. They didn't see any use in it. In the ecclesiastical world of Chichester there was no money in art. They liked the drawings and were entertained; but they saw no future in it save that of a 'poor artist'. This was all to the good. It was a disinterested activity as far as I was concerned and no one thought of it otherwise. So for the next few months (it seemed much longer – but months are years to the young) I drew the cathedral, from every point of view, and all its doors and windows and pillars. I cycled about all round the countryside, going home in the dusk of the evening with my bag of catches. And churches had shapes, because they had forms. The form was what mattered, though I knew it not.[5]

4   *Ibid.*, p. 83.
5   *Ibid.*, pp. 83–4.

His diary for 1898 is full of the record of his exploration of the Cathedral: '16 May – finished St. Richard's Walk for Mr. Catt; 16 June – sketched Cathedral Library and St. Richard's Walk; 10 September sketched S.W. door in the morning; 14 September – S.W. Tower morn.; 23 December – walked around vaulting with Mr. Moore.'[6] But soon Gill's period of exploring the city, of 'life in fairyland', of discovering drawing, had to come to an end. Now he was to meet three people who were to influence the rest of his life. As he confessed in his *Autobiography*:

> Then, after a while, I suppose they thought I had had enough freedom and ought to be doing something regularly and definitely. My memory of that time is of a constant activity of drawing, but I expect the truth is that I spent a lot of time idling about and being a nuisance…I think I had periods of moody selfishness and gaucheness. I don't think I was any help at home. I was being spoilt – the budding 'artist' to whom the other children must look up and for whom 'allowances' must be made. So my father took me round one evening to see the master of the Art School and told him that I wanted 'to embrace a career of art'. The phrase embarrassed me, but I certainly wanted to do something definite and was very glad to be taken on as a whole-day student at the Chichester Technical and Art School.
>
> Then began a period almost equally divided between rapture and rebellion. I worshipped the art master [George Herbert Catt]. Everything he said was right, and everything he did. He represented the good and the true and the beautiful. I hung on his words and followed him about like a dog. On Sunday afternoons he took me for walks in the country. He pointed out all the beauties of nature and taught me all about the styles of medieval architecture and how to tell the dates of buildings and he quoted Tennyson's *In Memoriam* at every turn ... And then we went back to tea in his little Queen Anne house – Sunday afternoon tea and toast, the glow of firelight and the glow of spiritual fires.[7]

The Record Office collection includes a couple of letters that Gill wrote to Robert Heaps, a lay vicar at the Cathedral, in which he describes a holiday in North Devon that he shared with Catt, which ended in their visiting Exeter Cathedral. Also in the collection is a drawing by Gill of Bideford Bridge. You can imagine my delight when I was asked by one of Catt's family to choose some of his pictures for the Record Office a couple of years ago, as I came across a view of the same bridge by George Herbert Catt. Both drawings are now in the Record Office and I like to think that master and pupil created them together.

> And I worshipped at the art school too. But there things after a time became difficult. The art master made me go in for 'exams', and I had to prepare great sheets of drawing – plant life drawn with extreme accuracy, and meticulously

6 Gill's diary, William Andrews Clark Memorial Library, UCLA. Copy at Tate Gallery, London.

7 Gill, *Autobiography*, pp. 84–6.

'shaded' drawing of cubes and blocks and other art-school 'properties', examinations in 'perspective'. And it gradually transpired that I was destined to be an
'art-master' and that all these examinations were to that end. I worshipped my
teacher but somehow or other my acquiescence in his plans became less and less
enthusiastic. I didn't see myself like that. It was all very well to get medals and
prizes (I never got a medal but I did get a thing called a 'Queen's Prize' – that
was in the days of Queen Victoria – for perspective drawing) but it was quite a
different matter to spend your life in the 'South Kensington' art-school world. I
began to like the prospect less and less.[8]

In his diary, Eric Gill recorded his first commission in 1897, when he was
15 – 'Mr. Firth gave me for sketching his church for his Mag. 7/6d.' Mr Firth was
vicar of Portfield Church in Chichester. Unfortunately no complete copies of
his Parish Magazine have survived in the Record Office. There is a fragment of
a 1901 Magazine which includes this drawing of the church. Other early patrons
recorded in his diaries were Mrs Wilberforce, the wife of the Bishop of Chichester, who purchased drawings from him in 1898, and commissioned Christmas
cards, and a Mr Frampton who paid him for painting his book. Among the
drawings in the Record Office Collection are three panels relating to the tomb
of the Countess of Arundel in the Cathedral which Gill entered for the National
Book Prize from Chichester College of Art in 1900. The same year saw his first
published design, for which he won the National Competition for Art Schools.
It was a design, submitted from Chichester for a 'card plate' for visiting cards,
to be carried out in pottery, with an apt inscription – 'Fresh as the first beam
flickering on a sail that brings our friends up from the underworld'. His diary
records that he started the design in November 1898.

Fortunately at this crisis point, when he had determined not to become an
art-teacher, Gill met Dr Robert Henry Coddrington, the Cathedral Prebendary,
who lived at 2, St Richard's Walk. In an anonymous recollection of him published
after his death, the writer declared: 'Dr. Coddrington was a saint; he would have
been distressed to hear himself so called and would have repudiated it emphati-
cally, for a more humble man never lived.' But there was no disguising the fact
that he was a saint. Gill described him thus:

> Meanwhile, in addition to the art master, I had made another friend and found
> another angel of enlightenment – or, more accurately, I had been befriended
> by him and taken under his wings. For, though the drawing and 'sketching' and
> art-school classes may be said to have occupied all my time, there grew up in
> the interstices a great enthusiasm for church music, for going to the Cathedral
> services and sitting in the choir stalls. I suppose I did this almost every day, I

8 *Ibid.*, pp. 86–7.

was as regular as any canon and much more regular than any lay person except the usual Cathedral lunatic. I made friends with all the choir boys (and played football with them) and the lay vicars, and then a great day came when I was asked to tea by one of the Prebendaries. I was already very great friends with the head verger or sacristan and under his instruction I learnt all the odd gossipy history which is the mainstay of that profession. But he was a truly grand old man, his deep loving-kindness to young boys and old stones made him as much more than a mere 'cathedral guide' as a bishop is more than a man and a priest – he was more than a guide, he was also counsellor and friend, and he seemed to have been in some way consecrated. He allowed me to have the keys of the doors and I got to know the cathedral in its very bones – all the mysterious circular staircases and dark places – over the vaulting – I climbed the spire and walked all the clerestories and galleries. I knew my way about as well as the masons and much better than any of the clergy. I haven't got much of a head for high places but I dared myself to a lot of dangerous and very silly adventures and I made drawings in all sorts of odd places and listened to the music through holes in the bosses of the vaulting.[9]

His surviving drawings of the Cathedral include a view from the south which he sent to his future father-in-law as a Christmas Card, as a fifteen-year-old boy his first Christmas in Chichester; a view of the Cathedral from St Richard's Walk the following year; another view of the same dated 1900; and yet another which came to light as a result of an exhibition; a view of the top of the South West Tower of the Cathedral in 1900; a view from West Pallant, also of 1898; an interior of the South Aisle looking towards the font of 1900; a view of the Retrochoir looking towards the Lady Chapel of 1900; and a view of the Arundel tomb in the South Transept. And it is surely true that when he was sketching the Cathedral he fell under the influence of the famous Chichester reliefs of the Raising of Lazarus and Christ's arrival at the house of Mary and Martha.[10]

But Gill's idyllic life in Chichester was not destined to last, and readers of recent biographies will not be surprised to learn that the reason for the idyll coming to an end was the fairer sex. First the object of his affection was a fellow art student:

So my two years of Chichester came to an end, but not before I had 'got over' the art-school love affair and had really and truly fallen in love with the daughter of my old friend the sacristan and, on the strength of the grand future which loomed up before me as a London architect, had actually proposed marriage and been accepted.[11]

9   *Ibid.*, p. 87.
10   For the significance of this relief see below *Chapter Four*, pp. 40–1.
11   Gill, *Autobiography*, p. 90.

Before speaking about Gill's marriage and his subsequent attachment to the city, he demands to be heard again on the influence of George Herbert Catt on his later career:

> But at Chichester, under the influence of the art master I discovered that letters were something special in themselves and, urged by his enthusiasm I became expert in inventing what seemed to me later the most monstrous perversions and eccentricities in the way of 'new art' lettering. I could almost wish I had that freedom now. And yet we weren't really free; for we laboured under the tyranny of art-school fashion — a harder master because more capricious than any 'tradition' or than any such rational notion as that the primary business of lettering is to be legible. Lettering was a part of art-school 'art'; its primary business was to be what they called and still call 'decorative'. But though I am ashamed of it now, I was jolly proud of it then, and my prowess was highly esteemed and earned me much undeserved praise. The 'really important' thing, however, is this: that I was, in a not too inaccurate manner of speaking 'mad' on lettering, and this, though I never dreamed of it at that time, led to a complete change in all my ambitions and the wrecking of all the castles in Spain built for me by my kind friends and relations.[12]

Chichester still boasts some examples of Gill's lettering. First is the stone tablet in the south transept of Chichester Cathedral in memory of Percy Joseph Hiscock, five years a chorister and five years a bell-ringer at the Cathedral; which is only the second inscription he ever cut, in 1900. Then, almost next to it, is the alabaster tablet in the Cathedral in memory of his father-in-law Henry Holding Moore, for forty-four years sacristan in the Cathedral. And then there are two gravestones in Chichester Cemetery: one to his father-in-law and family in 1931, and the other to John William Madden of the Royal Sussex Regiment in 1937, which Gill designed and David Kindersley cut. There are also two examples in the Record Office collection: a name-plate for a house in Worthing of his sister-in-law Mrs Walters, and a magnificent alphabet with incised letters and in relief.

Gill may have left the city — his family had moved to Bognor in 1899 and he left the Art College in the following year — but his heart was still there, because of his continuing interest in its doings and in its form and in the person of Ethel Mary Moore his future wife.

His love for the city manifested itself in his well-known and topical interest in the future of the Market Cross. Gill naturally drew the Cross when he lived in Chichester; he also intervened in a lengthy correspondence about the proposed restoration of the Cross, with two characteristic letters he wrote to the *Chichester Observer*. In the first, published April 1901 he wrote:

12 *Ibid.,* p. 91.

With reference to the proposal to restore the Chichester Market Cross as a memorial to her late Majesty Queen Victoria, I take the liberty of asking you a few questions and making a few remarks on the subject that have occurred to me. My chief desire in writing to you is to know whether it is proposed to restore or to repair the Cross; for there is a great difference between the two. I take it that restoration means the renewing of a building stone by stone, so that it may appear to be again what we suppose it originally was; whereas to repair a building is to keep it by every means in our power constructionally secure, both as a whole and as regards detail. To do the first would surely be a mistake. For what satisfaction do we obtain from all the examples which surround us of the restoration of old buildings and monuments which have been done during the last 80 years – the years of the Gothic revival? They are certainly not specimens of medieval masoncraft, but strike us rather as caricatures of medieval inspiration [...] Chichester Cross is one of the few remaining specimens of ancient art still left more or less in its original condition. In Bishop Storey's time, the English mason's craft was perhaps at its highest pitch, and the beauty of the work is astonishing to us. The Cross has suffered much from weather and decay, but so also have the pictures of the 16th century painters, yet who but vandals would think of repainting them? I fear, however, that this is practically what it is proposed to do to Chichester Cross. It is intended to renew or replace all the ornamental parts, which have fallen into decay, with new stone, carved as we suppose it was carved in the year 1500. Is it not absurd to imagine that 20th century workmen can, however skilful they are, transport themselves back into the 16th century and do the work which only exists at all because the 16th century existed?

Of course, it must not be forgotten that, unlike an old painting, a building, as it decays, becomes insecure and is in danger of altogether collapsing. We must at any cost prevent such a fate overtaking our Market Cross. This brings me to my second point, that of repair. The stability of the structure must be repaired by every means in our power. But only those stones should be touched which are necessary to the actual safety of the building. If it be found necessary to replace carved stones, let us cut them to our own design, shaping them so that they will harmonise with and carry on the old weathered stones on either side. Such work would be no deception, and passers-by would be able to see at a glance where repairs had been done. But let us not try to imitate the inimitable. Do not let us pretend to be Gothic workmen when we are not.[13]

Significantly Gill signed his letter, 'A Cicestrian in London'. The controversy rumbled on. Two years later a Mr Firth Bailey wrote to the *Chichester Observer* suggesting that the Cross should be carefully taken down and rebuilt either in the Cathedral yard or in the centre of Jubilee Park. Gill could restrain himself no longer, and wrote again to the paper:

13 Walter Shewring (ed.), *Letters of Eric Gill* (London, 1947), p. 17ff.

Re the letter signed Firth Bailey in your issue of last Wednesday, January 28th. 1903, I think the suggestion made therein an exceedingly brilliant one and very feasible indeed. Why, if I remember rightly, a great many fine old buildings have been ruthlessly pulled down, some of which have most certainly been rebuilt and some – not. There was the case of the Bell Tower at Salisbury, demolished because it was in the way. Though I never heard that it was rebuilt in any park – Jubilee or other. But if Chichester Market Cross was pulled down and erected in Chichester's Jubilee Park what a useful thing it might become! It might easily be converted into a band stand where the Chichester Brass Band might delight the ear of Cicestrians on a summer's evening, and if it were not considered large enough the upper story might also be used, and with the help of a cast-iron and glass and bric-a-brac canopy supported on atrocious cast-iron columns it might be made a most handsome and edifying spectacle. On the other hand if the Cross was rebuilt within the Cathedral yard it would undoubtedly be a great convenience to visitors to our city – from the point of view of economy – as all photographs of the Cathedral might then have the Cross thrown in.

But, Sir, I have never seen the press of traffic so great as to constitute the Cross a serious obstruction, although I admit it sometimes takes five minutes to get round it – by the clocks. But are we Cicestrians, as a rule, so pressed for time that we mind that? However, if in the struggle for existence our old Cross must be cleared away, why, having got it safely down, should the poor Cicestrians go to the expense of rebuilding it? For having once been pulled down the Cross would have no historical or other interest whatsoever, however carefully rebuilt. Indeed it would then matter little what were done with the materials, whose interest lies in their having been built together on that spot in the centre of the city more than 400 years ago.
I am, Sir, your etc. A Cicestrian in London'.[14]

On 4 August 1904, at the age of 22, Eric Gill married Ethel Moore, in his father's old church, St Peter the Great or Subdeanery in West Street, Chichester. The *Chichester Observer* has a full and fascinating account of the occasion:

The Church of St. Peter the Great was the scene of an interesting wedding on Saturday afternoon last, the contracting parties being Mr. Eric Gill, eldest son of the Rev. A. T. Gill of St. John's Church, Bognor, and Miss Ethel Moore, eldest daughter of Mr. Councillor H. H. Moore, Chichester. The approach to the altar was appropriately decorated with white flowers, and during the arrival of the numerous friends of the bride and bridegroom, Mr. Osmond Daughtry, Organist of Christ's College, Cambridge, skilfully rendered a pleasing selection of nuptial music on the organ, from Haydn, Corelli etc. The bride was escorted into the church by her father, and was attired in a dove coloured voile dress with a Brussels lace veil (which was worn by her mother) with a wreath of myrtle, carrying a shower bouquet of white flowers. She was attended by her sister, Miss

14   *Ibid.*, p. 20ff.

Violet Moore, as bridesmaid, who was dressed in pale green voile, and black picture hat, carrying a shower bouquet of cream roses. Mr. Max Gill, brother of the bridegroom acted as best man. The first part of the service was taken by the Vicar, the Rev. J. Spencer Walker, after which the Rev. Dr. Coddrington, conducted the principal part of the ceremony, the concluding portion being read by the Rev. A. T. Gill, father of the bridegroom. At the conclusion of the ceremony, as the bridal party left the altar, Mr. Daughtry effectively played Mendelssohn's Wedding March. A reception was afterwards held at the residence of the bride's father, which was attended by a large number of relatives and friends after which Mr. & Mrs. Eric Gill left by the 5.4 train for London.[15]

There followed a delightful description of all the wedding presents. I will give just a taste — 'Mrs. Arnold, ostrich feathers' [The list is in alphabetical order] Mr. Arnold, silver jackal skins, Miss Arnold, silver mustard pot; Miss Marjorie Arnold, silver mustard pot spoons; Mr. & Mrs. Brablington, silver tea spoons and sugar tongs; Rev. Dr. Coddrington, cheque; The Misses Carter, cushion', right down to 'Miss Wild, fancy slippers.'[16]

When the Gills caught the 5.4 train to London it did not signal the end of Eric Gill's association with the city. We know from his letters and diaries of his visits to see his family and friends, the artistic commissions he carried out in the vicinity, and of his desire to return. After their stay in Hammersmith, both Eric and Ethel, later named Mary, Gill contemplated moving back to Chichester. Gill and Edward Johnston discussed returning there together to establish a Chichester *scriptorium*. But in fact they decided to move to Ditchling and never returned to the city.

When he came to write his *Autobiography* in 1940, some 40 years had elapsed since Gill had actually lived in the city, and his memories of those few years had taken on a rosy glow. But Chichester to Gill meant the beauty and order of a Roman city; the magnificent stone sculptures in the Cathedral; the musical traditions of the Cathedral; and his awakening to the beauty of nature, of art, and of buildings. The retrospective vision of his nostalgic autobiography may in places be somewhat suspect but for Eric Gill Chichester remained 'something as human as home and as lovely as heaven'.

In 1950 Mary Gill, Eric Gill's widow, and Walter Shewring, his literary executor, visited Chichester with a view to establishing a permanent collection of Eric Gill's work in the city. The basis of the collection was to be formed from bequests by Mary Gill, Walter Shewring, Evan Gill, Eric's brother, and Fr Desmond Chute, once his apprentice and always one of his dearest friends.

---

15   *Chichester Observer and West Sussex Recorder*, 10 Aug. 1904.

16   *Ibid.*

Walter Shewring made the first deposit in 1952, with a drawing of one of the BBC sculptures, and, in the following year, Eric Gill's widow presented a number of engravings, being engravings from Geoffrey Chaucer, *Troilus and Criseyde* (Fig. 2), which formed the basis of the collection. Dr Olive Gill presented a number of books which had belonged to her husband, Archdeacon Romney Gill; and the executors of Mgr John O'Connor presented an important group of engravings. By April of that year, the collection was sufficiently established for it to be declared open for public exhibition by the Mayor of Chichester, and an exhibition was held in the room adjoining the main Assembly Room. The collection was considerably enlarged in 1963, when Walter Shewring, as representing Fr Desmond Chute, presented a large selection of books, together with a few original drawings and some woodcuts, including his ordination card of 1926, and Joan Hague, Eric Gill's daughter, presented some original drawings and the first of the small sculptures, a Madonna by Eric Gill painted by Fr Desmond Chute, *c.*1919. (Plate 1).

The collection had now become substantial enough to necessitate a move from the Council House to the new City Museum. In 1964 the City Museum organised a highly successful exhibition of Gill's work based on the Chichester Collection, but also including a number of items from private collections. However, the very success of the exhibition caused problems for the future of the collection. The Museum Committee, which was hard pressed for space in its new Museum, had to admit that they were short of the necessary storage space for the material, which was continually growing with new items forwarded by Walter Shewring and Evan Gill. Finally, after the exhibition had closed, the Museum Committee announced that it could no longer accept any further additions to the collection. After lengthy negotiations with Gill's executors the collection was transferred to the County Record Office. In 1967 the County Record Office published a catalogue of the whole collection, edited by Noel Osborne, just before a collection of small sculptures was received and a number of original drawings from Laurie Cribb's family. John Skelton, Gill's nephew and last apprentice, described the Chichester Collection in an essay in the book published to mark *Chichester 900*, as covering 'every facet of Gill's multifarious creative activities, woodcuts, wood-engravings, and pamphlets, title pages, life drawings and drawings of buildings.'[17] The Record Office continued to collect the considerable literature on Gill and his work and in 1982 celebrated the centenary of Gill's birth with a second edition of the catalogue which included all the material that had been deposited since 1967.[18]

17   John Skelton, 'Eric Gill and Chichester' in Walter Hussey (ed.), *Chichester 900* (1975), pp. 48–52.
18   Timothy J. McCann (ed.), *The Eric Gill Collection at Chichester. A Catalogue* (West Sussex County Council, 1982).

A number of significant deposits have enriched the collection since that date. After the death of Rene and Joan Hague, the Record Office received a number of personal papers including Gill's scrap books, his army papers, title deeds of the various properties he owned, family baptism and marriage certificates and wills, as well as Gill's London box which he took with him when he travelled to London from Capel or Piggots. When Walter Shewring died, he bequeathed to the Record Office a number of books and articles as well as a few engravings and an original drawing. What made the bequest even more valuable was that he had studied the catalogue very carefully and had tried to fill the gaps in the Record Office holdings from his own collection. Finally, the Record Office was able to purchase a number of items at the sale of the Hague collection. The present catalogue, available on computer and on-line, lists a thriving collection that is now more than twice the size of that catalogued in 1967.

2   Eric Gill's conversion: a key document in Ditchling Museum of Art+Craft

Joe Cribb

The year 2013 is important for Eric Gill studies. It is not only the year of the centenary of his conversion to Roman Catholicism, but also of the reopening of Ditchling Museum after an extensive rebuild funded by the Heritage Lottery Fund and numerous private and trust fund donations. The museum will reopen as the Ditchling Museum of Art + Craft with displays focused on Eric Gill and the artists and craft-workers who followed him to Ditchling after he made it his home in 1907.

One hundred years ago this year Gill moved to a new house just outside the village of Ditchling. It was here that he laid the foundation of the Catholic community which became formalised as the Catholic Craft Guild of St Joseph and St Dominic.[1] The Guild was founded in 1920 with his fellow craftsmen, Hilary Pepler, Desmond Chute and Joseph Cribb. All members of the Guild became Dominican tertiaries and said the Divine Office together in their own chapel. When Gill moved to Wales from Ditchling in 1924 he left behind him a strong heritage of craft making in the village. The newly opened museum will display works by Gill and his associates, both those who were members of the Guild and others, such as the calligrapher Edward Johnston, who made Ditchling their home.

Gill's conversion to Catholicism on 22 February 1913 was the conclusion of a long process already being contemplated by Gill in 1911 as recorded in a letter to his friend William Rothenstein.[2] After this correspondence and other conversations with his friends, he met with various priests and began formal instruction. His own account of his conversion, written almost thirty years later, was however more poetic. In his own words Gill, rather than joining it, 'invented the Roman Catholic Church'.[3] He grew up the son of a clergyman who had

---

1   For the work and the influence of the Guild, see below *Chapter Three*.
2   Walter Shewring (ed.), *Letters of Eric Gill* (London, 1947), pp. 41–3.
3   Eric Gill, *Autobiography* (London, 1944), p. 190.

gone through his own process of conversion, from a non-conformist sect to becoming a member of the Church of England. Religion therefore always played a role in Gill's life, and change must have seemed part of the process of spiritual growth.

When Gill left home in 1900 he moved to London and relished the intellectual atmosphere of the city. Even after he moved to Ditchling in 1907 Gill continued to engage with artistic and political circles in London. A letter in the collection of Ditchling Museum of Art + Craft documents Gill's rejection of these former interests as he made his first formal approach to seek instruction regarding his becoming a Catholic. The letter lists the history of former attachments to the modern 'faiths' of the city: the Arts and Crafts movement, Socialism (the Fabian Society) and the new theologies (Wells and Shaw particularly):

> *From AER Gill, Letter Cutter & General Carver, Mason, Etc.,*
> *Ditchling,*
> *Sussex.*
> *January 18th 1912.*
>
> *Dear Mr. Meynell,*
> *I understand that you are a Catholic — will you forgive me therefore for my presumption in writing — and, if so, you are the only Catholic with whom I have had personal dealings. My father is a Church of England parson and so, until I was old enough to read Huxley & H. G. Wells & Co., I was a protestant. Since the age of 17 or thereabouts I've wandered among the 'new arts' & the 'new religion', and new politics too, and have been as enthusiastic as could be expected. But I've got through the Arts & Crafts. I've got through the Socialisms & I've got through the new theologies. At the same time there is something in them all which is right. They are all revolts against the present devilish state of England. It seems to me from what I can learn & also guess that the Roman Catholic Church is the right answer to Modern England & also to Morris & also to Wells & Shaw & also to the Campbellites & Besantites & Anglicans & all the rest.*
>
> *But how can I find out? I know no Catholics to speak to. I don't want to bother you to convert me — even if I were worth it — but can you of your charity just tell me to whom such a one as I can apply to for information, instruction and enlightenment? I hope you won't think it a bother.*
> *Yours sincerely,*
> *Eric Gill[4]*

---

4 Ditchling Museum of Art + Craft, Evan Gill Collection. (First published by Robert Speaight in, *The Life of Eric Gill* (London, 1966), pp. 61–2.)

The addressee of the letter was Everard Meynell a member of a prominent Catholic family who owned a shop selling devotional books and art in central London. Gill met Meynell in 1911 when he was commissioned by him to create a monument for the grave of the Catholic poet Francis Thompson at St Mary's Catholic Cemetery, Kensal Green in North London.[5] Two letters from Gill agreeing the terms and details of the commission are also in Ditchling Museum of Art + Craft's Evan Gill Collection. Meynell's answer directed Gill to his father Wilfrid Meynell who prompted Gill to visit Fr King at St Etheldreda's church, Ely Place, in central London. Wilfrid Meynell invited him to stay the weekend at Greatham in Hampshire. Gill started attending Mass and met again with Fr King and Abbot Ford, the Benedictine Prior of Ealing. His visit to the Benedictine monastery at Louvain in May 1912 was also an inspiration and he started reading the works of the Catholic writer G.K. Chesterton. Later in 1912 Gill began to receive formal instruction from a Canon Connelly in Brighton, where he and his wife were received into the Church on 22 February 1913.[6]

This was also a key year for Gill's development as an artist, as he began the process of gaining his first large sculptural commission. This was the Stations of the Cross for Westminster Cathedral, a huge undertaking which took him nearly five years to complete. His conversion and perhaps his friendship with the Meynell family appear to have played a part in his being given the commission. The day after he got it he wrote to Everard Meynell with the news: 'You'll be glad to hear that I have got the commission. I am.'[7] His new faith also influenced his more intimate art as in 1913 he made his first wood engraving of the crucifixion (Fig. 3) and his first carving of the crucifixion with a Catholic theme. (Fig. 4).

Gill's January, 1912 letter to Everard Meynell not only reveals his journey towards Catholicism, but also evidences his inclination for belonging to movements and organisations. Although his entry into the Catholic Church ended this period of searching, Gill still had a taste for being part of an organisation. In 1919 under the influence of Fr Vincent McNabb, Gill joined the Third Order of St Dominic and in 1920 became a founding member of the Guild of St Joseph and St Dominic. Later in life he also became an active participant in the pre-Second World War peace movement.

The letter also mentions his engagement with the 'New Religion', essentially a form of spiritual humanism. Although soon abandoned, the New Religion with its emphasis on the centrality of mankind had a profound influence on his development as a sculptor, as well as shaping his approach to Catholicism. In the name

5   Evan R. Gill, *The Inscriptional Work of Eric Gill* (London, 1964), no. 219.
6   Speaight, *The Life of Eric Gill*, pp. 60–67; Fiona MacCarthy, *Eric Gill* (London, 1998), pp. 112–115.
7   Ditchling Museum of Art + Craft, Evan Gill Collection, 9.4.1914.

of the New Religion he began working with Jacob Epstein in 1910–11 on a modern Stonehenge to be located in the Sussex Downs for which he carved a large relief of a couple making love, *Ecstasy*, (Fig. 5) while Epstein started his *Maternity* sculpture. This brief association with Epstein brought Gill into contact with the latest trends in art developed by the *avant garde* in France, and encouraged him to see his 'direct carving' of sculpture as something revolutionary.

Gill's *Ecstasy* sculpture was the inspiration and model for his *Divine Lovers* (Fig. 7); representing the visualisation of Christ as husband to the Church his bride. Gill saw this concept as central to his Catholic faith, embracing the imagery of Christ and his bride as first imagined by St Paul (*Ephesians* 5, 22–33) and elaborated by the mystic poet St John of the Cross. For Gill the *Song of Songs* from the Old Testament also represented the same idea:[8] 'the bride is in love with the husband and his Bride is in love with Christ. I am a member of that mystical body and share her ecstasy.'[9] In 1934 he expressed the same view in a more forthright manner in a letter of advice to a young friend contemplating becoming a Catholic: 'Joining the Church is not like joining the ILP [International Labour Party] or the 3rd International. It's like getting married … The church is the whole body of Christians – the bride.'[10]

Gill explored this idea in his art throughout his career and his writings reveal the religious thought behind his otherwise startling sculptures and engravings; for example, Fig. 6. The survival of Gill's correspondence at Ditchling Museum of Art + Craft and in other collections helps to piece together the narrative of Gill's relationships, his progress as an artist, and his development as a Catholic thinker. It is fortunate that Eric Gill was such a prolific letter writer and in several institutions, as well as at Ditchling, many of these letters survive. Their survival owes much to his brother Evan's assiduous collecting and documentation of his work. The refurbished Ditchling Museum of Art+Craft has extended its facilities to enable visiting scholars to do research on its reserve collections, library and archival material, and so become an important centre for Gill and related studies.

---

8 Ruth Cribb & Joe Cribb, *Eric Gill, Lust for Letter and Line* (London, 2011), pp. 98–105.

9 Gill, *Autobiography*, p. 192.

10 Cf., Rayner Heppenstall, *Four Absentees* (London, 1960), p. 26, where the full and somewhat explicit nature of this simile may be read.

3

Posters in the Eric Gill Collection at the University of Notre Dame[*]

John Sherman

The chapter which follows below highlights the influence of Eric Gill and other members of the Guild of St Joseph and St Dominic, especially Hilary (Douglas) Pepler, as reflected in the posters produced by St Dominic's Press, under the auspices of the Guild, to promote the work and ideals of those associated with it.

History of the Eric Gill Collection

The University of Notre Dame holds amidst its various collections over 2,600 items of Eric Gill's work, which includes books, pamphlets, broadsheets, prints, greeting cards, calendars, sketches, woodblocks, photographs, and other formats. Additionally, the Eric Gill Collection includes many examples of the work by men who either worked with or were apprenticed to Eric Gill, including Hilary Pepler, Philip Hagreen, Joseph Cribb, David Jones and Desmond Chute. The collection has most of the imprints of the Golden Cockerel Press (which produced *The Four Gospels*, with engravings by Gill). The posters and other additional output from St Dominic's Press, established by Hilary Pepler, are a distinguishing feature of the Notre Dame collection. Also included in the collection are hundreds of fine art prints and over one hundred photographs of Gill's sculptures.

The Eric Gill Collection was acquired in 1965 from John Bennett Shaw (1913–1994), a 1937 graduate of Notre Dame. Shaw was secretary-manager of the Bennett Drilling Company in Tulsa, Oklahoma; he also pursued a passion for literature and books, which he did through the Tulsa Book and Record Shop of which he was owner-manager. He obtained much of his collection from Eric's brother, Evan. In a foreword for a catalogue produced on the occasion of a 1978

---

[*] The following is an edited version of the publication, *Posters Held Within the Eric Gill Collection University of Notre Dame*, organized by University of Notre Dame undergraduate students Melissa Bagniewski, Shannon Brown, and Sara Cloon under the direction of Professor John Sherman of the Department of Art, Art History, & Design.

...gh Library Special Collection's exhibition based on the Gill Collection, tells of how he came to collect Gill's work:

> I believe that my first exposure to the work of Eric Gill was when I acquired Chesterton's pamphlet *Gloria in Profundis* [Gill did the wood engravings]. Somehow I had developed an appreciation for book illustration, though I had no training in art and no ability whatsoever in any creative aspect thereof. Further, I had developed an interest in the English Catholic writers from Hopkins and Thompson down to the then present Chesterton, Baring and Belloc. Later I read and collected Waugh, Greene and Knox. In the next few years I secured many Gill items as well as the best collecting tool of all – a bookshop. Through my interest in Gill I began to collect and to stock in my store the works of the Golden Cockerel Press, Hague and Gill, the Cuala Press of Ireland, and many other fine presses. After thirty exciting and expensive years I held a very extensive collection of Gill, The Golden Cockerel Press, G.K. Chesterton, and some eighty other specialties.[1]

Shaw corresponded frequently with Philip Hagreen, who had been a member of the Guild of St Joseph and St Dominic for a portion of his career. Through the relationship Shaw had with Evan Gill and Philip Hagreen, the University of Notre Dame was ultimately able to acquire the foundation for a truly unique collection. The library has continued to add to the collection since its original acquisition over forty years ago through purchasing books, prints, and miscellany as its budget would allow.

Hilary Pepler and St Dominic's Press

Harry (Hilary) Douglas Clark Pepler (1878–1951), was raised a Quaker; he converted to Catholicism in 1916 through the influence of Eric Gill and Fr Vincent McNabb, OP. He was baptised at Hawkesyard, the Dominican priory, by Fr McNabb. After his conversion he changed his name to Hilary. Pepler enjoyed numerous interests and had various career paths; he is mostly remembered for founding St Dominic's Press. His other interests included poetry, writing on social issues, mime and puppetry; on one occasion he was given an invitation to represent England at an international congress of puppetry in Liège.

In 1915 Pepler, then living in Hammersmith, set himself up as a publisher. His books appeared over the imprint 'London, Hampshire House Workshop, Hammersmith.' Later that same year he moved to Ditchling to join Eric Gill who had gone there some years previously. At Ditchling Pepler set up his own printing office with the assistance of Gill and Edward Johnston, this became

---

1   *Posters Held Within the Eric Gill Collection University of Notre Dame* (Notre Dame, 2012), pp. 2–3.

known as St Dominic's Press. Pepler was possessed of a special kind of genius for designing posters and title-pages for books. His first printing press was a one hundred-year-old Stanhope hand-press. He also had a double-crowned Albion Press ('double-crowned' refers to the British paper size standard of 20x30 inches) and a double royal Imperial Press (30x44 inches) for posters. Pepler wrote: 'My first poster was distinguished by a basket of flowers which we worked with four inkers – one for the black and three in charge of the colours which they dabbed on the 'flowers', lifting out the blocks after each impression.[2] He enjoyed a close friendship with G.K. Chesterton and became managing-director of the *G.K. Weekly* following Chesterton's death in 1936 – the same year Pepler retired from St Dominic's Press. Pepler and others members of the Guild of Saint Joseph and Saint Dominic frequently advertised in the *G.K.Weekly*.

The Hampshire House Workshops, Hammersmith

During the late 1800s Hammersmith, situated on the north side of the river Thames and west of London, was the home of many well-known artists; among them were Frank Brangwyn (1867–1956), who would later move to Ditch-ling; William Blake Richmond (1842–1921), Mary Anne Sloane (1870–1961), and Muirhead Bone (1876–1953). The Arts and Crafts movement was represented too, particularly by those involved in the book arts. Thomas James Cobden-Sanderson (1840–1922), established the Doves Bindery at No. 15, Upper Mall in 1893; later, with Emery Walker (1851–1933), he formed Doves Press at No. 13, Upper Mall, in 1900. The Doves Press eventually dissolved in 1909. William Morris (1834–1896), lived in Kelmscott House, 26, Upper Mall; he ran the Kelmscott Press, situated at No. 16, Upper Mall, 1891–98. Emery Walker, who lived a few blocks west along the river at No. 7, Hammersmith Terrace, was the owner of a photogravure business, located at No. 12, Upper Mall, which provided copper plates for both the Kelmscott and Doves Presses. The William Morris Society is currently located in the coach house of Kelmscott House; originally the home of the Kelmscott Press, it is now a private residence. (Fig. 8).

Hammersmith Terrace subsequently became home to a second-wave of creative energy: the calligrapher and type designer Edward Johnston lived at No. 3; the embroidery artist May Morris (1862–1938), daughter of William Morris, lived at No. 8; Edward Spencer (1873–1938), the Director of the Artificers' Guild Ltd workshop in Hammersmith, resided at No. 9. Hilary Pepler moved into No. 14, Hammersmith Terrace in 1905. In that same year Eric Gill and his wife Ethel

2 Hilary Pepler, *The Hand Press* (St Dominic's Press, 1934), p. 15.

moved to No. 20, Black Lion Lane, a short walk from Hammersmith Terrace. The architect Fred Rowntree (1860–1927) and the barrister Warwick Draper (1873–1926), also lived on Hammersmith Terrace, next to Pepler. Warwick Draper would later move into Kelmscott House.

Amid this *milieu* grew the Hampshire House Workshops, in Hammersmith Terrace, the origins of which lay in a club for working men established in 1907 by Douglas Pepler, Fred Rowntree and Warwick Draper.[3] Known as the 'Hampshire House Social Club', it was situated in an old house set in substantial grounds adjoining the garden of Kelmscott House, the former home of William Morris. (Fig. 9). Hampshire House was purchased with help from G.K. Chesterton, Hilaire Belloc and William Rothenstein.

The club was to provide intellectual and other forms of recreation for men twenty years of age and older. A contemporary description says: '…aiming towards the ideal of social brotherhood, with accommodation for Benefit, Thrift, Reading, Athletic and Friendly Societies, and the sale of 'Temperance Refreshments'. Open to religious and political discussions, it nonetheless held no attachment, formal or otherwise, to any particular religious denomination or political party. Douglas Pepler was the first honorary secretary. The club was supported by well-known personalities, the actress Ellen Terry being one of them. Hilaire Belloc's name appeared on the lecture list. An annual picture exhibition showed the work of local artists.

During the First World War the club gave hospitality and employment to a group of Belgian refugees who had arrived in London in 1914. These included a cabinet-maker, a skilled carpenter, a bootmaker, and skilled embroideresses. The club provided raw materials so that they might continue being employed in their trades. An exhibition was held in Burgess Hill (a village near Ditchling) in 1914 to provide aid for the refugees. 'The Slaughter of the Innocents', a wood-engraving by Eric Gill, was used for the catalogue cover.[4] The title most likely refers to the "Massacre of the Innocents of Ypres" – an early WWI battle (Fig. 10).

So as to maintain continuity and ensure that jobs undertaken were completed, directors were appointed to oversee each industry. The work continued after the refugees had been resettled, developing into the Hampshire House Workshops producing furniture, embroidery, and shoes.

Douglas Pepler developed the Hampshire House Workshops, at No. 6, Upper Mall, which formally took over at the end of 1916. He published 'A Statement of Aim Issued by the Founders of the Hampshire House Workshops Ltd', outlining their intent to establish small workshops to produce better quality goods and

3   Hilary Pepler, 'Hampshire House Workshop', *Blackfriars* 31:359, February 1950, pgs. 70–2.
4   Evan Gill, *Eric Gill A Bibliography* (Winchester, 1991), no. 309, p. 207.

provide better working conditions. The complete text follows, courtesy of the Donohue Rare Book Room, University of San Francisco.

Statement of Aim

Founders: Philip Burtt, W G Cruickshank, Harold T Ellis, Douglas W Rowntree, Charles Spooner, A M Cruickshank, Warwick H Draper, Douglas Pepler, Fred Rowntree, and Penelope Wheeler.

The Hampshire House Workshops Limited, registered under the Industrial & Provident Societies Acts, were founded by a group of persons who believe that small workshops are an asset of NATIONAL value because work can be done in them under better conditions than are possible under the factory system. In his own workshop a workman can design his work and carry it through to the end. Only under some such conditions is it possible for work to be done which will compare with that of the past, for which there is rightly so great demand. This demand is due to appreciation of a quality in design and workmanship rare in modern work and entirely lacking in work produced in the factories.

There is no reason that work of this century should lack these essential qualities. The present deficiency is not due to less competent human beings, but to the acceptance of the standards of speed and quality set up in the factory system and consequently to the incomplete and inadequate training of the modern craftsman. The Society has been formed to carry on handicrafts in a group of small workshops with the object of providing well made things from the best materials and of giving opportunities to men, women and apprentices to master a craft of their own choice under different and better conditions than are to be found elsewhere.

Small workshops have to be established to train MASTER CRAFTSMEN, MEN AND WOMAN WHO SHALL HAVE MASTERED A WHOLE CRAFT. Each workshop will eventually be made over to a master workman or put under his control. It is then hoped and intended to form TRADE GUILDS of Master Craftsmen and others to fix and maintain standards of quality and price, and be represented on the committee. Every member of the Society has one vote, irrespective of the amount of capital held. Interest will be limited to 5 per cent per annum.

A Dressmaking workshop, a Wood-workshop and a Bakery have already been started while a Printing and Publishing workshop is affiliated to the society.

The Dressmaking Shop
6, Upper Mall, Hammersmith

Except for a short period at the beginning of the year (1916) this shop has not lacked for customers during the two years of its existence. Miss Day, who is now in charge, will be pleased to show visitors examples of the work done. Gowns, blouses, coats and skirts are made to order. Embroidered collars, lingerie and clothes for children are in stock. (Plate 2).

The Wood Work Shop
7, Upper Mall, Hammersmith

The work done in this shop has been varied; two sets of bedroom furniture in sweet chestnut, dining room furniture in ash and oak, a lectern and panelled stalls for the apse of a church have been made. Repairs to the house in an adjoining property have been executed. The shop fronts and fittings have been made and fixed and structural alterations carried out at The 'Doves' Bakery and the workshop showroom.

The Doves Bakery
10, Upper Mall, Hammersmith

Bread, cakes and pastry are made and sold in the shop and delivered to customers in the neighbourhood. Trade has steadily increased. Bread made of English stone-ground flour is in demand. (Plate 3).

Printing and Publishing
Douglas Pepler, 2 Upper Mall, and Ditchling, Sussex

This workshop is affiliated to the Society but is financially independent. A list of the books, prints &c, published can be had on application.

Personnel
It is our object to establish these workshops with the minimum of capital, we do not wish to demonstrate how money can be spent but how things can be made. We still require £250 in order to have the £2000 we consider necessary to the proper establishment of the workshops. We also want to make things for people rather than for stock. Our enterprise can be helped therefore in two ways: (1) by the purchase of shares and by (2) the purchase of goods.
W.G. Cruickshank

The poster shown in Plate 2 is a perfect example of Pepler's design philosophy; in his *The Hand Press* he wrote: 'The poster should contain as little information as possible and that of the greatest moment. It should say one thing and supply only sufficient directions for getting it.'[5]

Eric Gill designed the "The Hog and Wheatsheaf" wood engraving in October and November 1915. (Fig. 11). In Gill's first drawing for the wood engraving, the location of the bakery was No. 10, Upper Mall, and then in later drawings the location was changed to Doves Place. 'The Bakery had no equal for bread and cakes in the borough, nor had it then been discovered that, despite the exuberance of its bakery bag with its Eric Gill woodcut, its bread was not sufficiently favoured locally to warrant extensions contemplated.'[6]

Posters for Lectures

As well as being a letterer and stone-carver Eric Gill was also in demand as a public speaker. On 14 February 1933 he gave a lecture at High Wycombe entitled, 'Catholic Principles & Unemployment.' (Fig. 12). The lecture was later revised and extended for inclusion in Gill's pamphlet *Unemployment*, published in 1933, in which he lays out an argument claiming that the increased adoption of labour saving machinery is causing unemployment and thus destroying the family. Gill concluded the lecture thus:

> I am not going to say anything about the blessings of machinery. The reader knows them as well as I do and better. And I am not going to tell anyone what they ought to do. My only business here is to put forward certain things called Catholic principles, things which we hold to be matters of common sense & human reason as well as of divine revelation (for it is God who made us and not we ourselves, and so human reason is a reflection of divine reason). And my business is to point out how those principles bear upon the problems which confront us in England to-day – and particularly the problem of machinery & the consequence of machinery – namely unemployment – that is to say the fact that as a consequence of the use of machinery an increasing number of human beings can never have a full-time job again.[7]

As is well known the Guild of St Joseph and St Dominic consisted of members of the Third Order of St Dominic and so had close relations with the Dominican Order. In the 1920s and 1930s the University of Cambridge held an annual Dominican week of lectures during the Lenten Term in the Guildhall,

---

5   Hilary Pepler, *The Hand Press*, p. 47.
6   Pepler, 'Hampshire House Workshop', p. 71.
7   Eric Gill, *Unemployment* (London, 1933), p. 25.

Cambridge. (Plate 4). How the posters for the lectures came to be printed at St Dominic's Press is probably through the close friendship of Fr Hugh Pope OP, with Fr Vincent McNabb O.P., a professor of philosophy at Hawkesyard Priory who sought to promote a vision of social justice inspired by Pope Leo XIII's *Rerum Novarum*. He was also a key figure in the formation of the Guild of St Joseph & St Dominic. He held strong views on the close link between the Catholic faith and life on the land as practised in Ditchling. Fr Hugh Pope was a frequent lecturer for the series along with Fr Hilary Carpenter O.P., and others. These lectures are discussed by Kieran Mulvey O.P. in 'Lectures and Controversies', in his book, *Hugh Pope of the Order of Preachers*. Examples of topics covered by him are: 'The Existence and Nature of God' (1926), and 'God, Miracles and Prayer' (1929). Fr Carpenter spoke on: 'Immortality of the Soul', 'Reason and Faith', and 'Conscience' (1929).[8]

Hugh Pope was born 5 August 1869 at Kenilworth, ordained a priest 19 September 1898, died 23 November 1946 in Edinburgh. He was assigned to Hawkesyard Priory in 1898 as a professor of Sacred Scripture and librarian. In 1914 Fr Pope was elected prior of Woodchester, here he began a course on open-air preaching which would later grow into a nation-wide movement known as the Catholic Evidence Guild. Following a second term as prior he was nominated regent of studies at Hawkesyard. When the theological studies were transferred in 1929 to Oxford he went to that centre, still as regent of both houses. In 1935 he returned to Hawkesyard as prior.

Hilary Carpenter was born 1 October 1896 at Cheltenham, joined the Dominicans at Woodchester in 1915, made his profession on 6 November 1916, and was ordained priest on 1 April 1922, he died on 18 December 1973. Fr Carpenter taught at Hawkesyard, where he was also estate bursar; in 1929 he was appointed student master at Oxford. After a short time back at Hawkesyard he was appointed prior of Oxford in 1934 for two terms. He edited the Dominican journal *Blackfriars* from 1934 to 1940.[9] Fr Carpenter served also as the Provincial of the English Province, and chairman of the Catholic Film Institute.

Both Frs Pope and McNabb were very active in the formation of the Catholic Evidence Guild, an organization that would proclaim the doctrines of the Catholic Church in public settings, most notably Speakers Corner in Hyde Park. Organizations such as this, the Catholic Social Guild and the Distributist League, helped spotlight the work being done in Ditchling and drew Catholic craftsmen to come and join the community. 'In due course other Catholic families and

---

8   Kieran Mulvey OP, *Hugh Pope of the Order of Preachers* (London, 1953), p. 133.
9   Simon Francis Gaine O.P., *Obituary Notices of the English Dominicans from 1952 to 1966* (Oxford, 2000), p. 61.

individuals settled in the same part of the Common sharing in various degrees the same antipathy to modern degradation and the same ambition to return to normal life; so that counting all the children & single adults there are now (Feb. 1922) forty-one Catholics living and working at this corner of Ditchling Common – not one of whom was there in the beginning of 1913. Married, 13; children (over 16), 3; children (under 16), 18; Single adults, 7'.[10]

The fact that several Dominicans, but notably Vincent McNabb, promoted Ditchling as a kind of exemplar for modern day living caused it to become, in Gill's words, 'a spectacle of Christian family life'.[11] This made it difficult for the Guild to carry out its work without constant interruption and was one of the reasons why Gill went to live in Capel-y-fin.

Distributism, an economic philosophy popular amongst some Catholics, was based upon the principles of Catholic Social Teaching expressed in the Papal encyclicals *Rerum Novarum* (1891) and *Quadragesimo Anno* (1931). G.K. Chesterton and Hilaire Belloc were among those who advocated Distributism as a third economic system separate from Capitalism and Socialism. Its key tenets were: workers should have ownership of production, individuals should be able to own their own land and property, and that a community not be controlled by a highly centralized state or financial elite.

The Distributist League was founded in conjunction with *G.K.'s Weekly*, a publication edited by G.K. Chesterton. The first issue was published on 21 March 1925 in London. Eric Gill moved to High Wycombe from Capel-y-fin in October 1928. Gill's coming to High Wycombe may be the reason a Distributist League Branch was formed there. The address of 28 Crendan Street, High Wycombe, as can be seen in Figure 13, was the meeting place for the Distributist League in the town.

---

10   Hilary Pepler, *Memorandum*, (Ditchling, St Dominic's Press), p. 2.
11   Lottie Hoare, *Philip Hagreen: A Sceptic and a Craftsman*, p. 55. Available at www3.nd.edu/~jsherman/hagreen/Hagreen

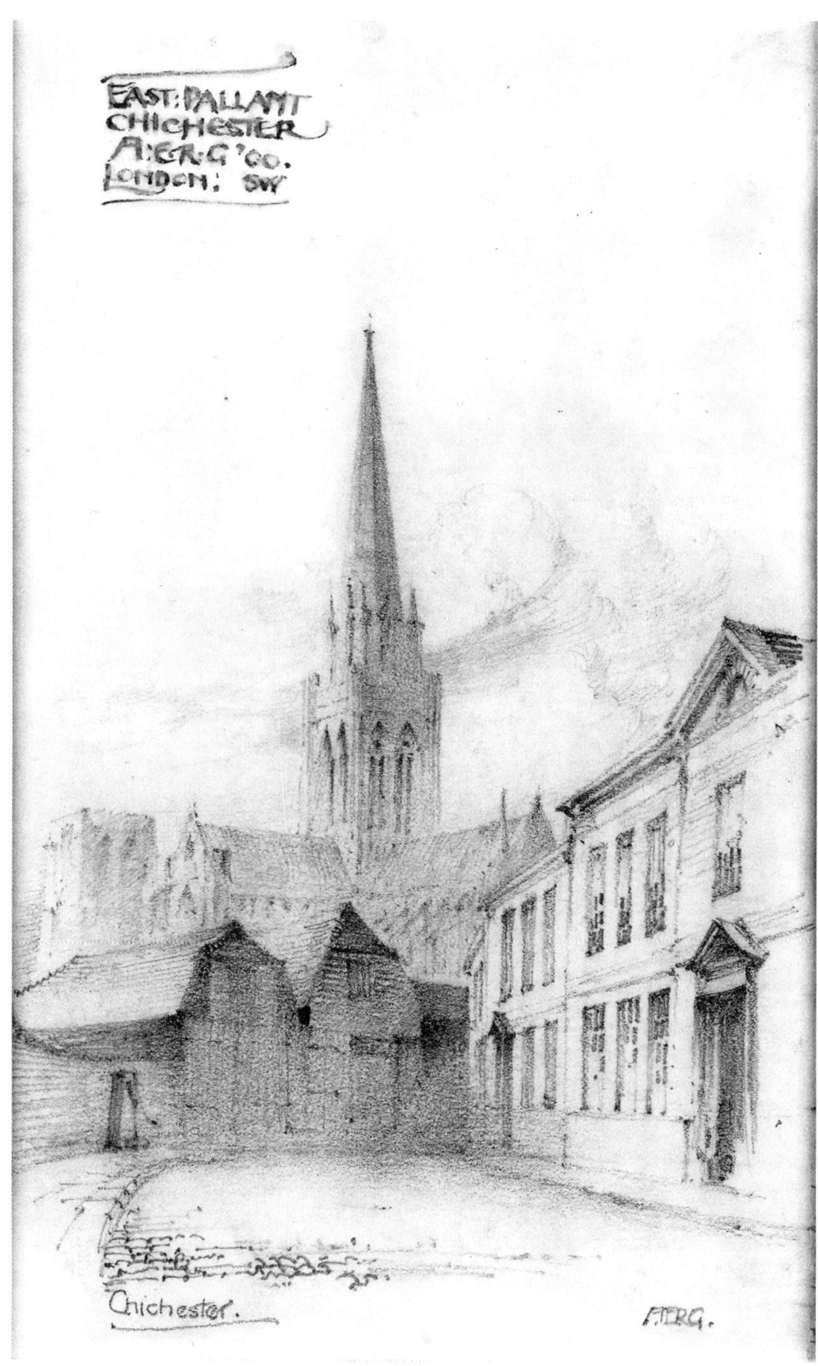

Fig. 1. *East* [recte West] *Pallant*, Chichester. Eric Gill, 1900.

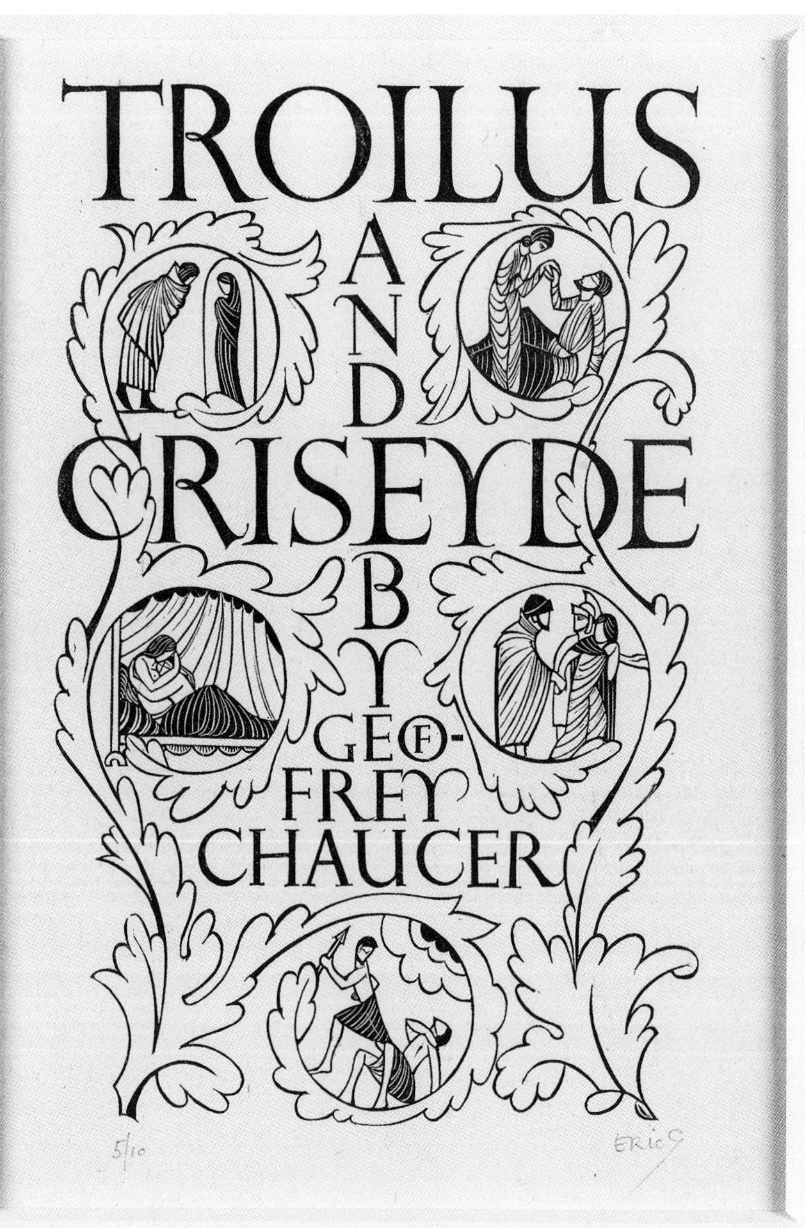

Fig. 2. Troilus and Chriseyde. Eric Gill, 1927.

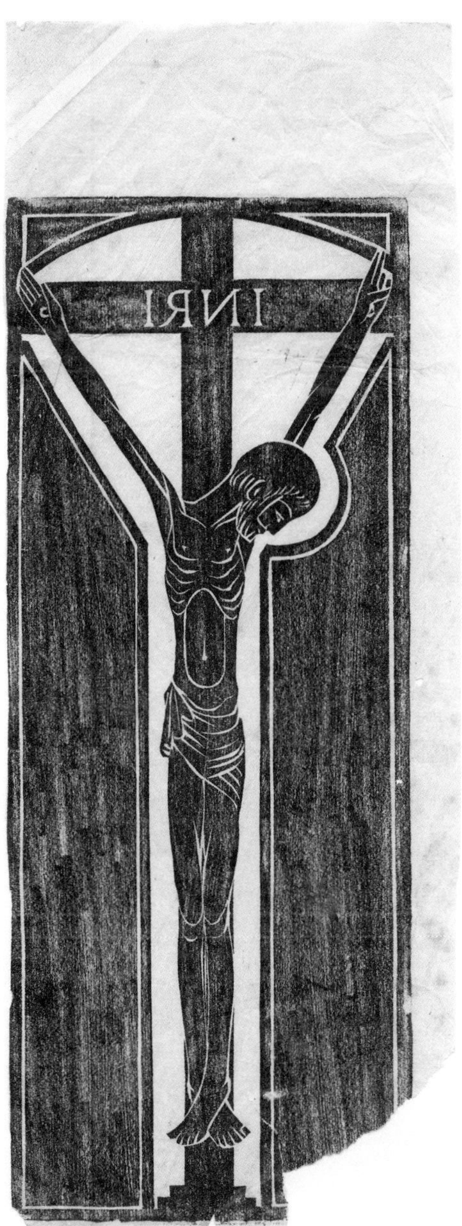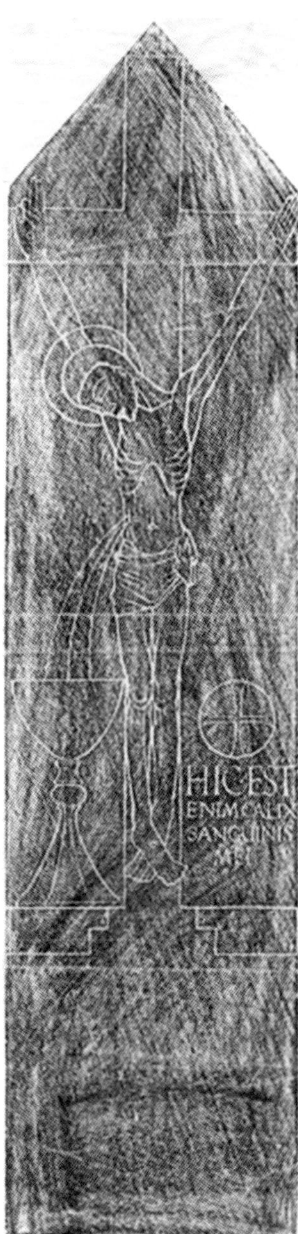

Fig. 3. [*left*] *Crucifixion*. Eric Gill, 1913. Rubbing of wood engraving, first state.
Fig. 4. [*right*] *Crucifixion*. Eric Gill, 1913. This carving was made by Gill from 11 April to 7 May 1913. On 8 May he took it to Everard Meynell's shop where it was put on sale. The design makes direct reference to transubstantiation. The image pictured here is an unpublished Gill sculpture which only survives as this rubbing.

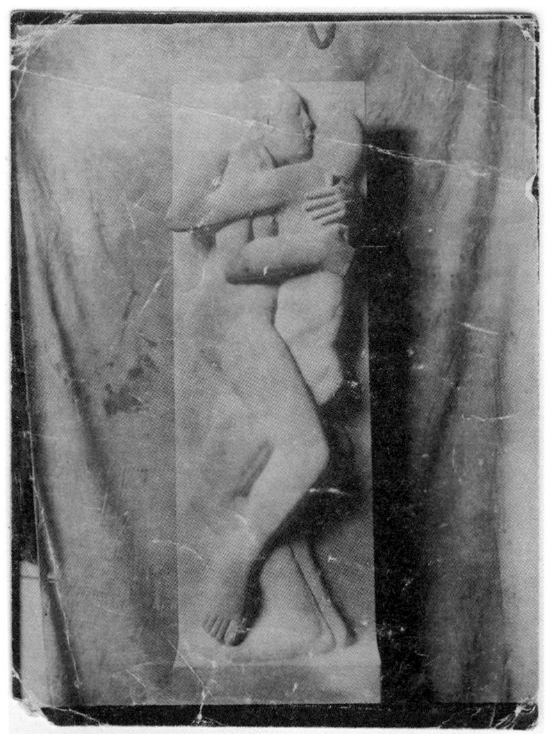

Fig. 5. Ecstasy.
Eric Gill, 1910-11.
Workshop
photograph.

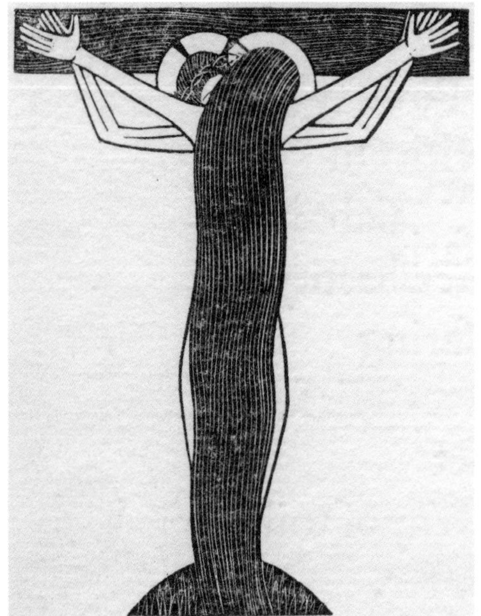

Fig. 6. The Nuptials of God. Eric Gill, 1922.

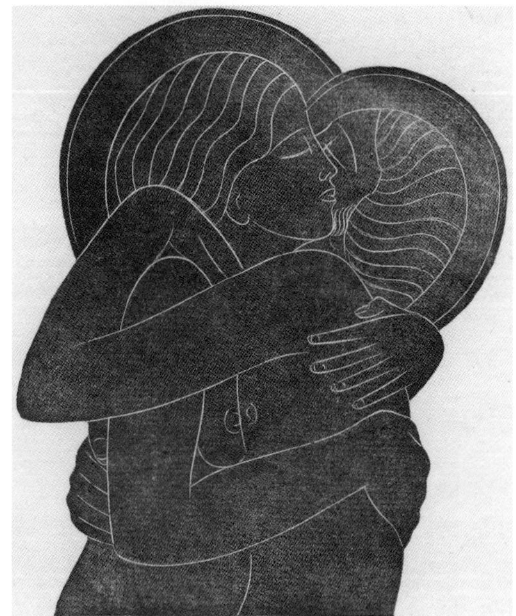

Fig. 7. Divine Lovers. Eric Gill, 1922.

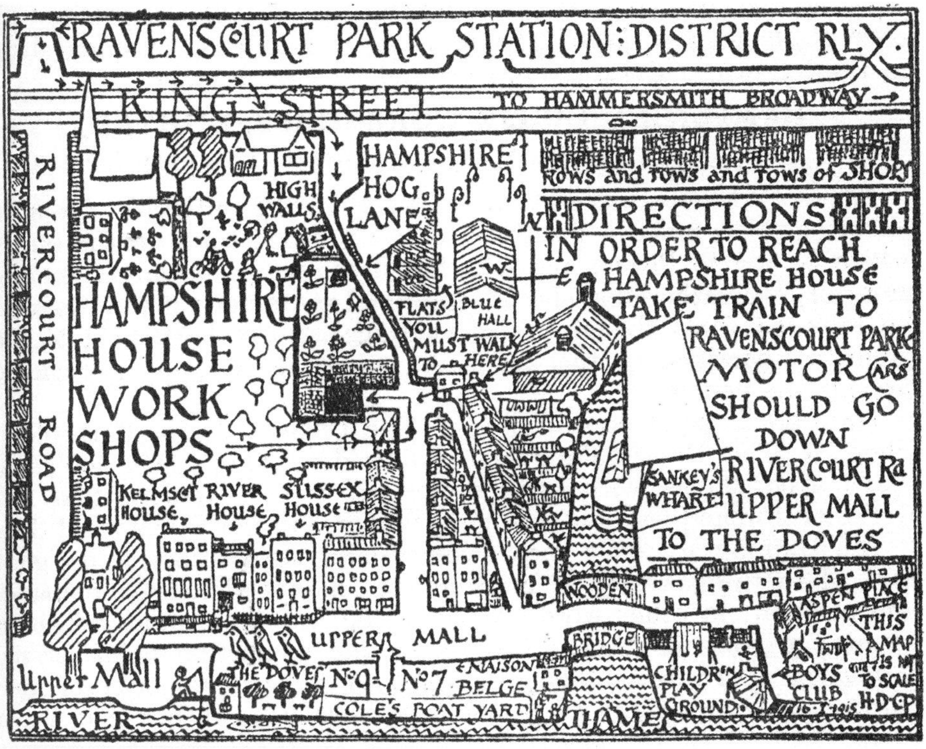

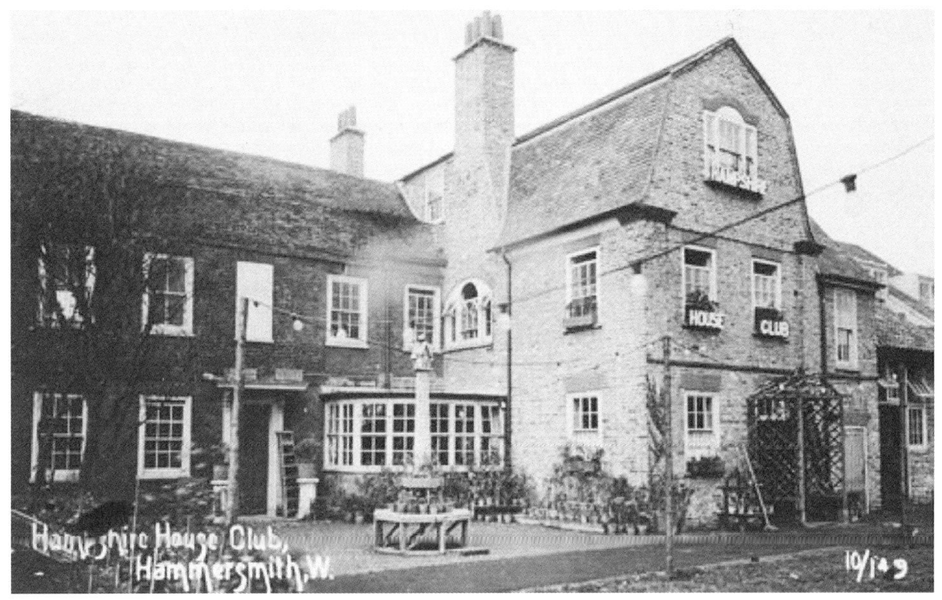

Fig. *8*. Hampshire House Workshop map 1915. Drawing by Hilary Pepler.

Fig. *9*. Hampshire House Club.

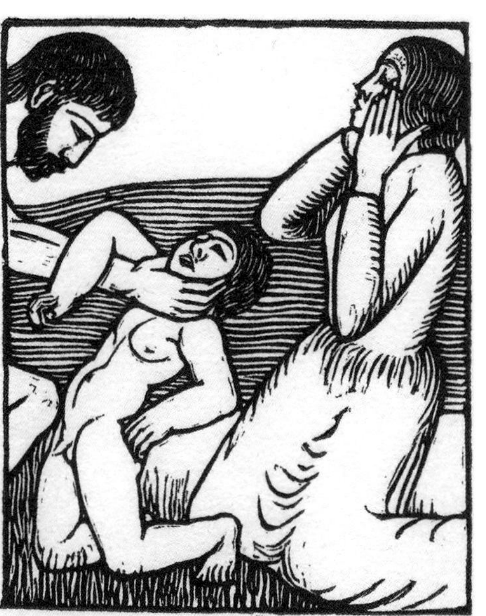

Fig. 10. Slaughter of the Innocents.
Eric Gill, 1914. Woodcut.

Fig. 11. Hog and Wheatsheaf. Drawing by Eric Gill
for wood engraving, 1915.

Fig. 12. Hague and Gill, 1933.

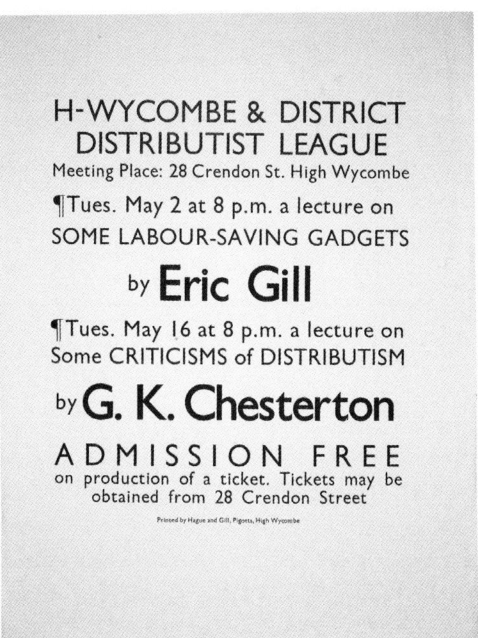

Fig. 13. Hague and Gill, 1933.

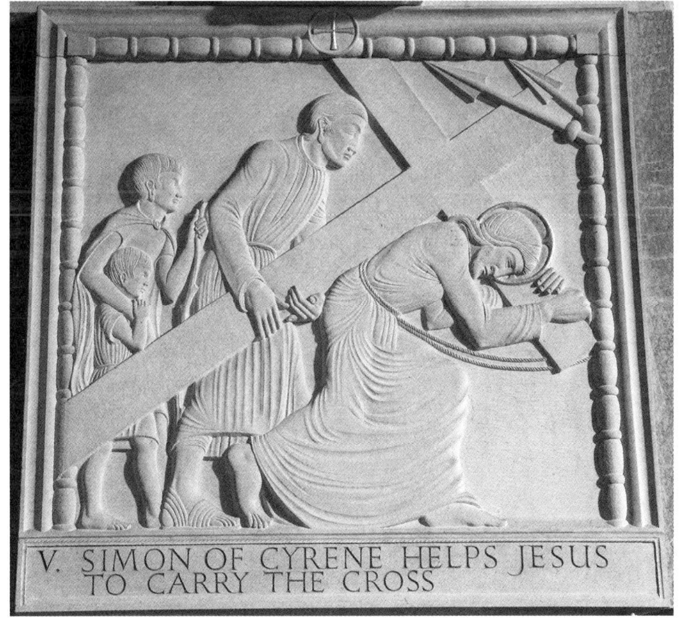

Fig. 14. Fifth Station of the Cross. Westminster Cathedral.
The composition is in reverse order to the trial panel (*Plate 5*).

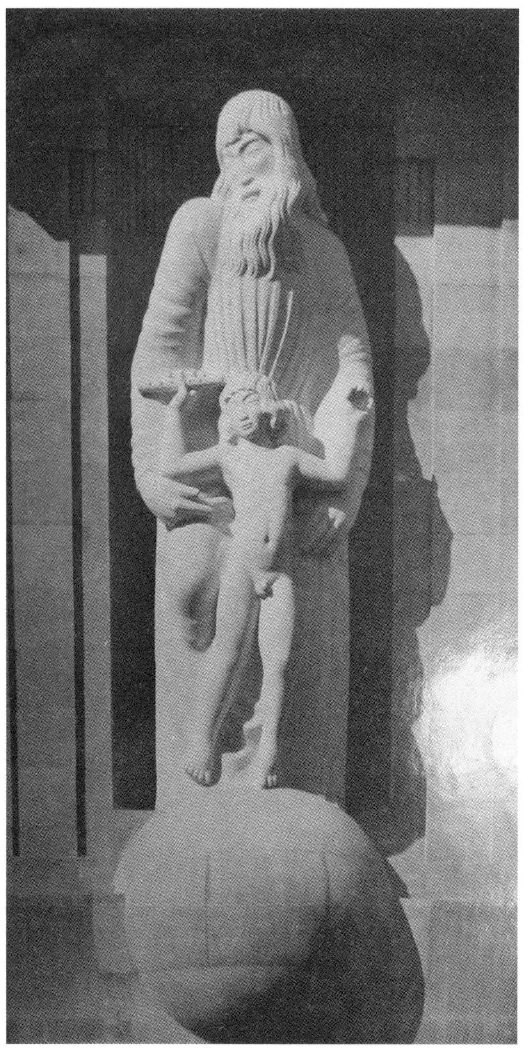

Fig. 15. *Prospero and Ariel*. Eric Gill, 1932–3. Broadcasting House, London.

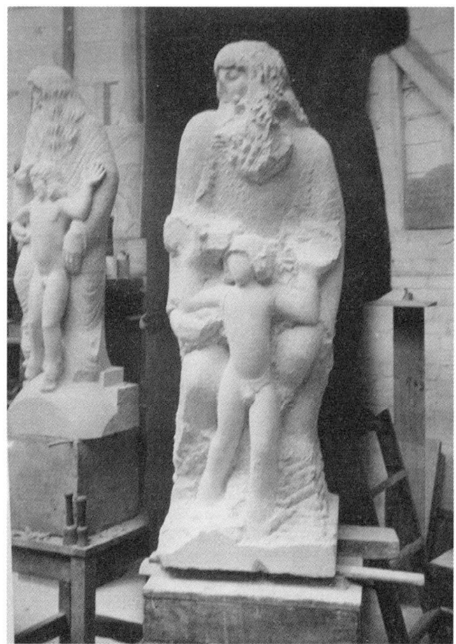

Fig. 16. [*above*] Eric Gill's workshop, showing the first and second models for *Prospero and Ariel*.

Fig. 17. [*below*] Model for *Prospero and Ariel* (later re-titled *Abraham and Isaac*). Photograph, after 1933.

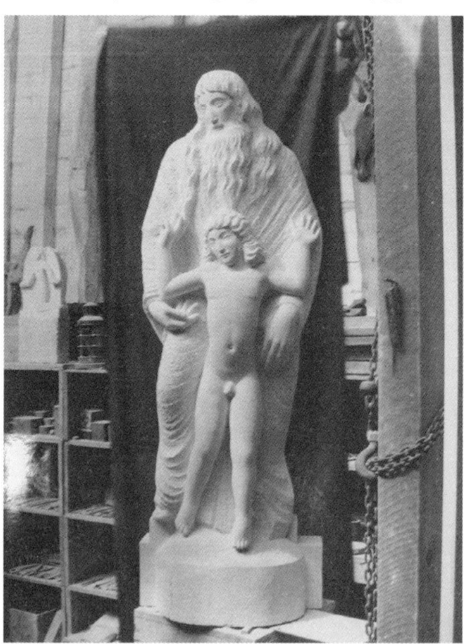

4

Conversion by Commission:
Eric Gill and the Westminster Stations[*]

Naomi Billingsley

In his written instructions, my husband expressed the wish for per[mission] to insert a small stone tablet about 9" square in the floor of the Cathedral under the 14th Station with the inscription: E.G. 1882–1940.[1]

In the floor under the fourteenth Station of the Cross in Westminster Cathedral there is a small stone tablet, which reads, in one of Gill's own letter-faces: *E.G. Lapidarius 1882–1940 R.I.P.* This unimposing tablet commemorates the quite extraordinary story of Eric Gill's Stations of the Cross (1914–18). It is a story which is significant in the history of the Cathedral, in the history of twentieth-century English church art and architecture, and in the career and thought of Eric Gill. For the Cathedral, the Stations are a monumental landmark in the decoration of its interior.[2] In the wider story of church art and architecture, Gill's Stations inspired a stylistic trend in English Stations of the Cross, a genre which was then still emerging.[3] Using material from Westminster Cathedral's archive, as well as published sources (especially Gill's own writings),[4] this chapter focuses on

[*] The permission of the Administrator of Westminster Cathedral to publish in this chapter material relating to the Westminster Cathedral Archive (hereafter WCA) is gratefully acknowledged. Thanks are also due to the Cathedral historian, Patrick Rogers, for reading the chapter on the Administrator's behalf. This essay has been developed from research undertaken towards an MA in Christianity and the Arts at King's College, London. I am grateful to the AHRC for funding this work. My thanks to Ben Quash for his comments and suggestions on earlier versions of this essay. Any errors and shortcomings are my own.

1 WCA, letter of Mary Gill to Mr Shattock [Cathedral Architect], 28 December 1940.

2 In the past two decades, the Stations have also been a source of controversy, following scandalous revelations about Gill's private life in Fiona MacCarthy's biography, *Eric Gill* (London, 1989), which raised questions for some about the appropriateness of having Gill's work in a church. No moral judgement on Gill's work is here assumed. As will be discussed, the Stations were also controversial at the time of production on stylistic grounds.

3 Stations reflecting Gill's influence can be found in various parts of the country, and would be a subject worthy of a comprehensive study.

4 The thesis of this chapter is supplied by evidence from Gill's diaries, which are held at the University of California at Los Angeles (UCLA), cf. p. 71, n. 91. Scattered extracts from Gill's

the significance of the Stations in the life of Eric Gill. He received the commission for the Stations in 1914 – the year following his reception into the Catholic Church; that he requested a memorial be placed below the fourteenth Station is telling: here, it is suggested that the Westminster commission was crucial in the development of Gill's thought on the ideas of Art and Beauty.

Westminster Cathedral

Westminster Cathedral, the Mother Church of the Catholic Church in England and Wales, was built at the turn of the twentieth century (1895–1903, consecrated 1910), designed by John Francis Bentley (1839–1902).[5] Bentley's plan for accommodating Stations of the Cross into his Byzantine design was to create them in *opus sectile*, a form of mosaic using flat pieces of coloured glass (much larger than the *tesserae* of ordinary mosaic and cut according to the pattern) to create the design, which is used in the decoration of two of the Cathedral's side chapels.[6] This plan was even announced in the *Westminster Cathedral Chronicle* in March 1909, inviting donors to give the £62 cost for one Station, and stating that one had already been given;[7] in October, it was announced that sufficient funds had been raised, but only empty marble frames appeared. Several years later, the Cathedral authorities were seeking alternative designs, and in 1914, decided on Gill, who would carve the set in low relief in Hoptonwood stone.[8] The Cathedral's archive provides some fascinating (and tantalisingly fragmentary) insights into the commission and its importance for the development of Gill's theology of art.

The Cathedral Archive

The archive is housed above the Baptistery, at the west end of the building, in the room which was Bentley's office whilst he was overseeing the project (it was the first part of the building to be completed). Thus, there is a powerful sense of the history of the building in the very location of the archive, enriching the

---

diaries quoted in biographies by Robert Speaight, *The Life of Eric Gill* (London, 1966) and Fiona MacCarthy *Eric Gill*, have been taken into consideration (as well as the overall accounts of Gill's life by these authors), some of which have been quoted.

5   John Browne & Timothy Dean, *Westminster Cathedral: Building of Faith* (London, 1995), p. 11.

6   On *opus sectile* in the Cathedral, see Patrick Rogers, '*Reflections: The Westminster Cathedral Mosaics* (London: Oremus, 2010), pp. 21–24.

7   'Editorial Notices', *Westminster Cathedral Chronicle* (March 1909), p. 62. Gill's Stations were sponsored by donors, recorded by plates below each Station.

8   Patrick Rogers, *Westminster Cathedral: An Illustrated History* (London: Oremus, 2012), pp. 80–1; *The Beauty of Stone: The Westminster Cathedral Marble* (London: Oremus, 2008), p. 65–6.

experience of searching through its contents. It holds architectural drawings and decorative designs dating back to Bentley's appointment in 1894, as well as correspondence and other records.

Over the past two decades a number of conservation grants from English Heritage have enabled improvements to the archive. The drawings were removed from their old wooden plan chests, inventoried, eased and dusted; some of the Bentley drawings also needed to be repaired. All the drawings were photographed for reference, given text paper covers, and re-housed in conservation-quality steel cabinets. In 2004, the present archivist, Miriam Power, began work at the Cathedral; a priority for the preservation of the drawings was to develop a search and retrieval system, where previously items had been misfiled, making the existing finding aid unreliable. In consultation with the Soane Museum, photographers were sought for a digitization project, although owing to lack of funding and scheduling considerations, it was another five years before the photography began. A copy stand was installed in the archive, and with photographers working intermittently over a period of eighteen months, two thousand of the drawings were digitalised and a cross-reference database created. Descriptions were then added to the database to create an enhanced finding aid which could be easily shared, annotated and amended by key personnel. Many drawings and sketches were previously unnumbered or unidentified; the new system addresses this and the database will provide the kernel of a complete drawings catalogue.[9]

Gill retained most of his drawings for the Stations of the Cross and later sold them to the Victoria and Albert Museum, where they can be viewed in the Prints and Drawings Room. These include preliminary studies (for hands, feet etc.) and scale designs.[10] The design Gill submitted to the Cathedral authorities in May 1914 is now in the British Museum, and can be viewed in the Department of Prints and Drawings.[11] Gill chose as his trial panel the fifth in the series – Simon of Cyrene helps Jesus to carry the Cross. The design illustrated in Plate 5 is his second drawing for the smaller trial panel of 4ft 6in square which he submitted for the approval of the Cathedral authorities in 1914. For the larger panel, he

---

9 Miriam Power provided this information about the archiving project.

10 Museum nos.: E.2989 to 3016–1923, E.192 to 207–1924, E.222 to 251–1924. The design for the twelfth Station of the Cross (E.3011–1923) can be viewed on the V&A's online collections database. Time spent consulting Gill's drawings at the Victoria and Albert Museum was crucial in informing my understanding of the development of Gill's designs, although less directly relevant to the thesis of this essay.

11 Museum nos.: 1920/1211.1. This and four other relevant drawings (1949/0411.23 and 1949/0411.22 [both recto and verso]) can be viewed on the Museum's online research pages.

reversed the compositions.[12] (Fig. 14). The drawing is held in the collection of the Manchester City Art Gallery and was formerly owned by the businessman and art collector Charles Lambert Rutherston (1866–1927) who donated his collection to the gallery to form a unique loan service for educational institutions in the region.[13] The trial panel itself is now in the collection of the Harry Ransom Humanities Research Center at the University of Texas at Austin.[14] The Cathedral archive does have a number of drawings by Gill for various projects, including for work never realised.[15] Other records held in the archive include correspondence (although much is now in the care of the Westminster Archdiocesan Archives) and press clippings. The archive also keeps a full run of the *Chronicle* and other versions of the Cathedral bulletin (the present being the *Oremus* magazine), providing a record of the activities of the Cathedral since the *Westminster Cathedral Record* began in 1896.[16] Together with correspondence relating to the Stations, the *Chronicle*'s reports have been valuable for this research (in particular, one article written by Gill under the pseudonym "E. Rowton" on completion of the project), although these are surprisingly few for such a large-scale project. For example, there seems to be no report explaining the decision to depart from Bentley's plan of *opus sectile* (perhaps because the authorities were wary of potential controversy). Also apparently absent are records of the donors for the Stations (although these are acknowledged in panels below the Stations themselves); it would be particularly fascinating to uncover any correspondence between the Cathedral authorities and those who had already sponsored the Stations after the change in style was announced, but none came to light in the course of undertaking this research.

12   Judith Collins, *Eric Gill: The Sculpture - A Catalogue Raisonné* (London, 1998), p. 84.

13   Cf. Sandra Martin, 'Rutherston, Albert Daniel (1881–1953)', *Oxford Dictionary of National Biography* (Oxford University Press, 2004; on-line edn, May 2009).

14   Collins, *op. cit.,* p. 84.

15   Gill's last carving, which was not quite complete when he died in 1940, was the altarpiece for the Chapel of St George and the English Martyrs. It depicts Thomas More and John Fisher before the crucified Christ. Gill included a monkey next to Thomas More; More had a pet monkey of which he was very fond, so Gill intended this to be a reference to the saint's humanity, and to be a caricature of our lowly status. However, when the altarpiece was finally installed in 1947, the monkey had been removed at the instigation of the Cathedral authorities. This provoked considerable controversy, with a series of letters from both sides appearing in the *Catholic Herald* on 7 & 14 February; 7, 15 & 21 March; 30 May 1947; 13 February; 5 March 1948. Cf. Collins, *op. cit.*, p. 119.

16   The *Chronicle* and other versions of the Cathedral bulletin are also available at the British Library.

Gill's Commission

Eric Gill had been received into the Church just fifteen months before the commission for the Stations was signed. He was also relatively new to the art of sculpture; he had no formal training in the art and had only been carving for a few years (his first exhibition was at the Chenil Gallery in 1911).[17] One might expect that the prospect of creating one of the most prominent features of the most important Catholic church in the country would be a daunting one for a newly converted Catholic and relatively inexperienced sculptor, but for Gill, the task seems to have inspired excitement rather than anxiety; when the commission was confirmed, he wrote in his diary, 'The work is mine. *Deo Gratias.*'[18] He later boasted to his friend Henry Atkinson, 'It is one of the best sculpture commissions one could have.'[19] Gill believed that he was 'the only possible person for the job', because he was willing to work for 'a price no really 'posh' painter or sculptor would look at,' as well as having 'a proper Christian enthusiasm…[and] sufficient, if only just sufficient, technical ability…;'[20] it almost seems that Gill believed the task was his by divine providence. The then Cathedral architect, John Marshall, seems to have told Gill in no uncertain terms that he was chosen as an economical choice,[21] which is confirmed by a letter in the Cathedral archive from Marshall to Mgr Jackman, secretary to Cardinal Bourne, which comments on the favourable sum of £771.15.0, 'Much less than the original estimate' (11 April 1914).[22]

In his *Autobiography*, Gill describes his two conversions – to Catholicism and to sculpting – alongside one another.[23] His statements about his conversion to Catholicism are characteristically idiosyncratic and forceful. For example, he described converting as like taking the train to Peterborough; he decided he would take that train and there were no further obstacles in the way (one wonders if trains were more reliable in the 1910s!).[24] A recurring theme in his *Autobiography* is that he 'invented the Roman Catholic Church,' by which he seems to have meant

17　Eric Gill, *Autobiography* (London, 1940), pp. 160–177; Judith Collins, *op. cit.*, p. 11.

18　Speaight, *op. cit.*, p. 72.

19　Walter Shewring ed., *The Letters of Eric Gill* (London, 1947), p. 64.

20　Gill, *Autobiography*, p. 200.

21　*Ibid.*

22　The sum includes Marshall's commission; the entry in Gill's job book at Ditchling is for £765 (MacCarthy, *op. cit.*, p. 171).

23　Gill, *Autobiography*, pp. 131–192. Gill missed a trick by not noting that as he converted to carving stone, he converted to the Church of Peter, the 'rock' (Matt. 16:18).

24　Eric Gill, *Engravings by Eric Gill: A Selection of Engravings on Wood and Metal representative of his work to the end of the year 1927 with a complete Chronological List of Engravings and a Preface by the Artist* (Bristol, 1929), p.11

that as he learned about the faith, he discovered that it was 'identical' with the faith he had 'invented.'[25] He also described himself as the Prodigal Son:

> I had been away, squandering my substance in riotous living – not with women and wine, though that would have been nice, but with riotous young minds and the wine of strong words–and now I was, in a manner of speaking, coming home.[26]

This homecoming was as an artist; it was through developing his thought on artistic principles that Gill believed he had 'invented the Church.' He considered the prevailing view of art to be utterly incompatible with religion;[27] for the art world, art was about the artist, the artwork was an end in itself, and popular phrases such as 'fine art' and 'art for art's sake' put the artist on a pedestal. For Gill, not only was this snobbery – or 'art nonsense',[28] as he called it – it risked setting the artist as a rival to God.[29] Gill's definition of art, repeated time and again throughout his writings, is as skill; he believed that all artistry – from portrait painting to cooking – was art, which should be understood not as a self-assertive activity, but as workmanship or service. The artist should not rival God but collaborate in God's creating;[30] thus, art is a religious, even cosmic act. Gill's thought here was deeply indebted to Ananda Coomaraswamy (1877–1947), a Ceylonese philosopher of art who was a mentor and lifelong friend.[31] Although Gill's *Autobiography* is written many years later, in 1940, the ideas he professes to have led him to his conversion are indeed present in his writings of the 1910s, especially, as will be discussed, in his thought on the Stations.

As the Stations began to be erected, a debate began in the press between critics who argued that the Stations were not in keeping with Bentley's design, or thought them strange, and others who defended Gill's work.[32] Gill worked on

---

25 Gill, *Autobiography*, pgs.170 & 190

26 *Ibid.*, p.171

27 *Ibid.*, p.173

28 Gill, *Engravings*, pp. 310–324

29 Gill, *Autobiography*, p. 173

30 *Ibid.*

31 *Ibid.*, p. 174; *Cf.* Ananda Kenish Coomaraswamy 'The Christian and Oriental, or True, Philosophy of Art', *Every Man an Artist: readings in the traditional philosophy of art*, Brian Keeble (ed.), (Bloomington, 2005), pp. 56–82; Rama P. Coomaraswamy, 'Introduction', *The Essential Ananda K. Coomaraswamy*, Rama Coomaraswamy (ed.), (Bloomington, 2004), p. 1ff.

32 The critical controversy has been traced by Patrick Rogers in *Westminster Cathedral: An Illustrated History*, pp. 82–3. WCA holds a selection of press clippings which give an insight into this controversy: *The Observer*, 3 Oct. 1915, 'Art & Artists: The Decoration of Westminster Cathedral'; *The Observer*, 10 Oct. 1915, 'Westminster Cathedral Decorations'; *Scarborough Evening News*, 5 Oct. 1915, 'Westminster Roman Catholic Cathedral: Important Decorations Commenced'; *Yorkshire Post*, 5 Oct. 1915. See also: 'Mr. Eric Gill' *The Burlington Magazine for Connoisseurs* 32, no. 179 (Feb. 1918), p. 81; 'Review: The Stations of the Cross in Westminster

the Stations in the years 1914–18. They were put up as he carved them; he worked in large part *in situ*. As noted, the *Chronicle* remained almost silent as the Stations were erected, where normally it reported the progress of decorative projects. Although these were the war years the *Chronicle* was published as normal, and gave relatively little attention to war matters, which might otherwise have been an explanation for the lack of comment on the Stations. The exception was an article in December 1915, reprinted from the architectural journal *The Builder*, which defended the Cathedral authorities against critics of the Stations, and urged commentators to reserve judgement until the scheme was completed.[33]

The most useful source for understanding Gill's thought on the Stations is an article which he wrote for the *Chronicle* when he had completed the project in 1918.[34] It was published under a pseudonym, 'E. Rowton' (Rowton being his middle name), owing to the controversy about the style of the Stations. Gill's veiling of his name seems to stem not from a desire to distance himself from the views expressed in the article but rather to distance the reader from prejudice against his name; indeed, he told his friend, Joseph Cribb, that it was 'rather amusing' to be writing pseudonymously.[35]

"Rowton" begins by dismissing objections to the style of the Stations; they were made for worshippers, not for art critics, and it is not for worshippers to concern themselves with criticism of the style. In so far as they are works concerned with Beauty, the measure should not be their superficial Beauty – what he calls 'loveliness' – but whether they open the mind and heart of the viewer to *perceive* Beauty. Beauty, for "Rowton," is an Absolute, and should not to be confused with 'loveliness', which is only relative to being loved.[36] The artist is not the creator of Beauty but rather a servant to Beauty.[37] This idea of Beauty reflects the objections to the contemporary art world cited earlier in connection with Gill's statements about his conversion. Whereas the art world sought to *create* beautiful things, "Rowton" suggests that the purpose of art is to *point to* Beauty. This does not mean that art should not be superficially beautiful, but simply that that 'loveliness' is not the measure of the artwork; rather, the measure is whether it succeeds in leading the viewer to perceive Absolute Beauty. The role of the artist is not annulled, but rather, that role becomes one of conforming his

---

Cathedral', *The Burlington Magazine for Connoisseurs* 32, no. 182 (May 1918), p. 204.

33   *Westminster Cathedral Chronicle*, v. 9, no. 12 (December 1915), pp. 236–38 (first appeared in *The Builder*, 5 Nov. 1915).

34   "E. Rowton", 'The Stations of the Cross in the Cathedral', *Westminster Cathedral Chronicle* 12, (March 1918), pp. 50–53.

35   Shewring, *op. cit.*, p. 192.

36   "Rowton", 'The Stations of the Cross', p. 50.

37   *Ibid.*, p. 51.

activity to this Absolute reality. This reflects an idea from Coomaraswamy, that art must be spiritual and not merely 'pleasing'.[38] Coomaraswamy's own definition of beauty was as 'the attractive power of perfection',[39] which may be the source of "Rowton's" idea of Beauty as an Absolute. However, the language is different, and seems to reflect quite distinctively that of the Catholic scholastic tradition: Aquinas called Beauty an absolute because he identified it as an aspect of the divine essence (*Summa Theologica* 1.5.4). This transcendent, theological idea of Beauty has frequently been identified in Gill's later thought, in his writings after reading Jacques Maritain's (1882–1973) *Art et Scholastique* (1920).[40] Gill read Maritain in 1922, and the importance of its influence on his thought from that time is unquestionable,[41] but that the language of Beauty as an Absolute – and also of God as Beautiful[42] – already appears in "Rowton's" article, suggests that Gill had a genuine debt to the scholastic tradition earlier than commentators have often implied;[43] it seems that Gill was already beginning to adopt a distinctively Catholic idea of Beauty by 1918.[44]

In "Rowton's" article, there might seem to be two models of how art is service: service to Beauty, and service to the prescriptions of the Church. However, if

38 A.K. Coomaraswamy, 'The Christian and Oriental', p. 67.

39 *Ibid.*, p. 59.

40 Jacques Maritain, *Art et Scholastique* (Paris, 1920), published in English as: *Art and Scholasticism with Other Essays*, trans. J. F. Scanlan, (London, 1946).

41 Cf. Gill, *Autobiography*, p. 208. Most significantly, he wrote an essay on Aquinas's definition of Beauty as *Id Quod Visum Placet* (ST 1.5.4) (1926), meaning 'that which pleases when seen,' which was written in the style of the *Summa*, and is clearly influenced by his reading of Maritain. NB. Although this title might seem to be in tension with the notion expressed in the 1918 article that Beauty is not superficial, the purpose of the 1926 essay is in fact to elucidate the meaning of the phrase as Absolute rather than superficial.

42 "Rowton", 'The Stations of the Cross', p. 50.

43 Rowan Williams, for example, seems to imply that reading Maritain marks a watershed in Gill's thought between a 'sophisticated...pre-modern, oriental and hieratic philosophy of art' inherited from Coomaraswamy, and a distinctively Catholic philosophy (or perhaps better, theology), marked by 'the vocabulary of Maritain' (*Grace and Necessity* [London, 2006], p. 46). Williams does acknowledge Gill's earlier contact with scholastic ideas through the Dominicans, but does not seem to suggest any direct influence of this tradition on Gill's own thought in this period. He may also misrepresent Coomaraswamy, who was himself deeply indebted to Aquinas, even writing an essay on the idea of Beauty in the *Summa Theologica* 1.4.5 (A. K. Coomaraswamy, 'The Christian and Oriental'), though without using the scholastic terminology of Beauty as an Absolute and therefore leaving open the question of Gill's use of that language (cf. Rowan Williams, *Grace and Necessity*, p. 45ff). MacCarthy does acknowledge that the Stations are 'an early and extreme example of his theories for coherence, his belief that in art and life it all goes together; the sculptures are very simply the fittings of the building with a certain sort of purpose.' (*Eric Gill*, p. 125).

44 Cf. p. 71, n. 91.

Beauty is a facet of the divine essence (as in the scholastic conception), then these must be two ways of expressing the idea of art as service to God.[45] For "Rowton", just as the artist's task is not to *create* Beauty, so he should not make his own theological judgements when presenting a subject prescribed by the Church;[46] rather, guided by the prescriptions of the Church, the artist will learn to *reveal* Beauty through his work.[47] He therefore made his Stations as neutral as possible – like plainchant music, the beads of the rosary, or 'a sentence without adjectives.'[48] He disliked existing examples of Stations because he believed that they had been infected by the 'modern habit of allowing and paying other people to do everything for us...people do not expect to discover their own emotions but must have [want] them provided.'[49] In order to allow the emotion to come from the viewer, he 'confine[d] himself to the bare necessities of the subjects', paring the content to a minimum, and making the expressions of the figures 'as far as possible impassive.'[50] He also chose not to include the crowd so that the worshipper could enter that role (an idea paralleled in the post-Vatican II practice of the congregation voicing the words of the crowd when reading the Passion for Palm Sunday and Good Friday).[51] Like the rosary, the Stations are merely an *aid* to devotion, and thus, the worshipper should view them as simply 'reminders of the Passion' and approach them 'desirous of Beauty rather than loveliness.'[52]

"Rowton's" humbling of the artist from self-assertion to service has quite a radical and paradoxical effect; it elevates the artist's responsibility from making 'loveliness', to showing the way to God. Thus, the artist's work is itself an act of

45   "Rowton", 'The Stations of the Cross', p. 51.

46   *Ibid.*, p. 52. He adds an anecdote that as he was working on the Stations in the Cathedral, people (especially, he adds, women) would ask him about the subject of the Stations and were confused at his reply that that was not his concern: 'Madam...the devotion of the Stations is under the special charge of the members of the order of Saint Francis. Ask them.'

47   "Rowton" writes analogously about carving *from* the stone, rather than carving 'imitations' in stone; just as he submits to Beauty and the Church, so too to the stone with which he was working. Gill would develop this idea into his way of working 'true to materials' (cf. John Rothenstein, *Eric Gill* [London: Ernest Benn, 1927], p. 14).

48   "Rowton", 'The Stations of the Cross', p. 53.

49   *Ibid.*, p. 52. Gill also saw this tendency in more dramatic church music, architecture, art, furniture, images. Gill did not approve of the decoration, calling it 'sham Byzantine ornamentation...bloody rot' (David Kindersley, *Eric Gill Further Thoughts by an Apprentice* [London, 1968], p. 44), and was in favour of whitewashing the interior (Malcolm Yorke, *Eric Gill: Man of Flesh and Spirit* [London, 1981], p. 204), although he praised Bentley's genius of designing a building which could be a place of worship first and decorated second, calling Westminster 'Bentley's great act of worship' (Gill, *Art Nonsense*, p. 15).

50   "Rowton", 'The Stations of the Cross', p. 52.

51   Ibid.

52   *Ibid.*, p. 53.

worship and therefore an intensely personal process, but must manifest itself in neutrality.[53] This is important for understanding why the Stations were so important for Gill, and it is evident in the manner in which he made his designs. He designed and carved the panels not in sequential order but as each appealed to him,[54] presumably reflecting his own devotional impulses. In addition, he used himself, his wife and his assistants as models for the subjects.[55] Gill may also have borrowed from other sources;[56] one in particular, which has been highlighted by both MacCarthy[57] and Collins,[58] may have had personal meaning for Gill: Station VIII, *Jesus Speaks to the Daughters of Jerusalem*, bears a striking resemblance to a twelfth-century panel in Chichester Cathedral of Martha and Mary kneeling before Christ at Bethany. Station VIII shares with the Chichester relief the composition of the women kneeling in the bottom left-hand corner, and Christ positioned in the centre, striding from the right-hand side to bless them. Gill's time in Chichester had had a profound impact on him; it was there that he developed an interest in architectural drawing, and above all, of churches, because he was fascinated by the meaning of churches as 'being in some way manifestations of public worship, a sort of architectural ikons...'[59] He probably also encountered a cast of the relief in the Victoria and Albert Museum in London;[60] he certainly visited the cast collection, and perhaps an encounter with this familiar piece provided inspiration for his design.[61] Gill's use of very personal models and

53 As he later wrote of his work on the Stations, '[t]he Catholic artist is...free to run on rails' (letter to *The Universe*, 7 December 1934, in *The Letters of Eric Gill*, Shewring (ed.), p. 318.

54 Cf. Collins, *Gill: Sculpture*, pp. 90–104.

55 Joseph Cribb's hands for Christ's in II (London: Victoria and Albert Museum [V&A], E.225–1924); Geering for the hands of a soldier in III (V&A, E.228–1924; E.229–1924) and for Simon of Cyrene in V (V&A, E.231–1924); Balshaw's hands for Simon of Cyrene's in V (V&A, E.241–1924; E.242–1921; E.243–1924); Mary Gill's hands for Mary's in IV (V&A, E.230–1924); himself for Christ in X (V&A, E.234–1924), and soldiers in Stations II (V&A, E.226–1924), III (V&A, E.227–1924) and IX (V&A, E.232–1924).

56 Cf. Collins, *op. cit.*, p. 20–21. For the influence of Chichester on Gill see above *Chapter One*; regarding his interest in church buildings cf below *Chapter Eight*.

57 MacCarthy notes that although Gill never mentions the Chichester reliefs in his diaries or writings, she was told by Philip Hagreen, who worked with Gill, that Gill spoke of them with deep feeling, stating, 'I have seen those stones many times, but never without tears.' (Philip Hagreen to Fiona MacCarthy, 28 Jan 1987, in MacCarthy, *op. cit.*, pp. 28–9).

58 Collins, *op. cit.*, p. 39.

59 Gill, *Autobiography*, p. 84.

60 Museum no. REPRO.1864–57. No record is available to confirm that the cast was on display at this time. I am grateful to Louise Collins of the Sculpture Section in the Department of Sculpture, Metalwork, Ceramics & Glass at the V&A for pursuing this enquiry.

61 Eric Gill, *An Essay on Typography. With a new introduction*, Christopher Skelton ed., 2nd edn (London, 1988), p. 24.

borrowed motifs may indicate that in the process of creating the Stations, Gill was performing for himself that which he demanded of the worshipper-viewer: to inhabit the subject of the Stations. Although this incorporation of personal motifs might seem to compromise the Stations' neutrality, Gill's non-naturalistic style meant that he did not replicate his sources, but merely took a form or gesture for his designs, and thus without his preparatory drawings, or knowledge of the Chichester relief, it is not immediately obvious that any of the subjects resemble figures from life or elsewhere.

Conclusion: Stations in Gill's career

Gill repeatedly came back to the subject of the Stations throughout his career. He made four further sets, one carved after designs by his friend Fr Desmond Chute for St Cuthbert's Church, Bradford (1920–1924),[62] a second for Our Lady and St Peter, Leatherhead (1925),[63] a third (incised rather than carved) for St Alban's Church, Oxford (1939–1940; completed from his designs after his death),[64] and the recently rediscovered set in sycamore wood for Dogmersfield College Chapel, Hampshire.[65] Gill also continued to draw the subject, and made a set of engravings after the Westminster Stations which were used in two devotional volumes, *The Way of the Cross* (1917)[66] and *Social Justice and the Stations of the Cross* (1939). Over time, Gill's ideas about the subject of the Stations seems to have shifted quite radically. At Westminster, he seems to have remained quite neutral on their meaning; this is quite remarkable in light of the fact that he carved them in the war years 1914–18 (and that the commission actually granted him exemption from military service), when the subject of the Stations would seem to be particularly resonant, but Gill professed complete indifference to the conflict, writing: 'I thought quite simply and quite honestly that it was no affair of mine.'[67] Just a few years later, he was willing to carve Stations which made the Roman soldiers into Tommies (for Bradford); but these were Fr Desmond Chute's

---

62 Collins, *op. cit.,* No. 104, pp. 118–119; No. 107, p. 120; No. 109, p. 121; No. 116, p. 125; Nos. 146–155, pp. 139–143.

63 *Ibid.* No. 161, pp. 147–148.

64 *Ibid.* No. 294, p. 224–225.

65 *Ibid.* No. 299, p.229 (states 'present whereabouts unknown'). This set is now in the care of the De La Salle Trust, GB, and has been researched by Br Michael Curran in *Chasing the Provenance of Eric Gill's Wooden Stations of the Cross*, (Lasallian Publications, 2011). Cf. below *Chapter Seven*.

66 The prayers for this booklet are said to be by Hilary Pepler (my thanks to Joe Cribb for answering this inquiry on behalf of the Eric Gill Society).

67 Gill, *Autobiography*, p. 202.

designs, and perhaps Gill still believed that he was simply submitting to the prescriptions of the Church in undertaking this work. However, in *Social Justice and the Stations of the Cross*, Gill is taking up his role as worshipper, as a member of the crowd supplying the emotion for the Stations, and his reflections are potent and political. This may mark a break with the neutrality which "Rowton" insisted upon, although Gill might have believed that his personal writings should not be confused with the work he produced for the Church (Gill was also carving the Oxford Stations at that time, and the volume was illustrated with the engravings after the Oxford designs), and that being the crowd in the Stations (as he was in *Social Justice*) remained a very different role from being the artist. These are questions which would merit further attention.

In conclusion: Gill's request that he be commemorated under the fourteenth Station, as recorded in his wife's letter in the Cathedral archive, is testament to the fact that he continued to believe that the Stations were a milestone in his career. This certainly had to do with the fact that they were his first major sculpture commission, and thus helped to launch his career in that medium, but it also seems that his process of reflecting on his work as artist of the Stations was formative in developing his ideas about Art and Beauty. Whilst working on the Stations, Gill was working out his new identities (which were really one for Gill) as Catholic and sculptor. Thus, it may not be too far-fetched to suggest that the Westminster Stations represent at least as important a stage in the development of Gill's thought as his meeting Coomaraswamy and his reading Maritain, because the commission prompted him to reflect upon the nature of Catholic art. According to "Rowton", Beauty is a 'stumbling block':[68] Gill would continue to seek a deeper understanding of this Absolute, but at Westminster he seems to have begun to realise how through his art he might be led, and to lead, to Beauty and to God.

---

68 "Rowton", 'The Stations of the Cross', p. 52.

Prospero and Ariel or God the Father and God the Son? Eric Gill and the meaning and making of the BBC sculptures

5

Ruth Cribb

Patronage was central to Gill's career and was one of the most important factors in his success and in the growth of his public profile. From his early work at the architectural practice of W. D. Caröe, to his work for the League of Nations in the 1930s, Gill relied financially and professionally on the support of private and public clients. Some of his earliest patrons included Count Harry Kessler, owner of the Cranach Press in Germany, the stationary shop W.H. Smith, and the artist and critic Roger Fry. This variety of client type, which continued throughout his career, enabled Gill to work in different media, at different scales and with varying degrees of public recognition. This chapter will look at one public patron in particular – the BBC – to explore the often complex relationships Gill had with his clients. By 1930, when Gill was asked to carve sculptures for the new BBC headquarters in central London, he was one of the most prominent sculptors of the day and seen to be typical of the 'modern' movement. For many in the press 'modernity' in sculpture meant the use of British stone, of the artist working directly on that stone without the aid of models or assistants, and a certain level of abstraction or simplification of form. Despite his prominence, as will be seen, his appointment to this prestigious commission was far from straightforward.

Gill's instructions in the commission were clearly defined by the BBC; the various working relationships at the centre of the building of Broadcasting House, however, meant that the process of reaching consensus on the chosen artist and the final decorative scheme was complex. Gill's relationships with his clients were usually amicable, and he saw himself to be a contractor completing the instructions of his patron. As will be seen, Gill's private and public statements on this role suggest complexity in his perception of himself as an artist, a craftsman and a contractor. I will propose that the strict instructions given by the BBC enabled Gill to work more freely, but that his discomfort with these boundaries led him to make later changes to the meaning of the sculptures to suit his own intentions. I will examine the background to Gill's commission, the press reception of his appointment, and the meaning of the sculptures created. The material referred to below comes from the BBC Written Archive in Reading, the Hesburgh Libraries at the University of Notre Dame, and from the main archive of Gill's personal and professional papers at the William Andrews Clark Memorial Library, UCLA.

The building of Broadcasting House was managed by a syndicate of subscribers who then sold the lease to the BBC; the head of the syndicate was one Robert Solomon. Initially the discussion about which sculptor should be commissioned was between him and Colonel George Val Myer, the architect. The sculptural decoration of the building was intended to include: three relief panels designed into the building; a large figure group to fill the niche above the main entrance; and some decoration halfway up the building underneath the central row of windows. The latter decorative carving was completed by a general sculpture contractor. Solomon's first choice to complete the panels and the figure group was a relatively unknown sculptor called John Smith. Solomon wrote to Smith saying that the idea for the central figure above the niche was 'one symbolising human development – progress, or anything you like. The smaller figure, still comparatively primitive, rising slowly upwards and forwards, the other one merely symbolising the energy'.[1] For Myer, his 'whole conception of the building is bound-up with, not only the right placing and the proportioning of the sculpture in relation to the rest of the lines and masses but above all in getting the right quality'.[2] Myer also sought permission to visit the studios of the sculptors Charles Wheeler (1892–1974), Maurice Lambert (1901–1964) and Charles Sergeant Jagger (1885–1934). The content and appearance of the sculpture was of prime importance to both men.

These discussions, however, were not received well by the BBC Board of Governors or the Director General, John Reith. A small exhibition at Solomon's house on 6 October 1930 was intended to allow all the stakeholders to review the proposed designs by all four sculptors. Reith expressed his dislike for Smith's work because he did not 'want the sculpture to be at all on Epstein lines'.[3] It is apparent from the correspondence that this reaction on behalf of the BBC had in fact ruled out early inclusion of Gill, who was seen to be an associate of Epstein. On 30 October 1929 Gill had met with the critic Herbert Read (1893–1968), and Mr Goldsmith and Mr Lambert 'of the BBC' to discuss the 'possibility of doing

---

1   BBC Written Archives S167/4/4. Robert Solomon to John Smith, n.d. *c.* 13 Jan. 1930. [BBC WA]
2   BBC WA S167/4/4. George Val Myer to Robert Solomon, 26 May 1930.
3   BBC WA S167/4/5. John Reith to Robert Solomon, 10 Oct. 1930.

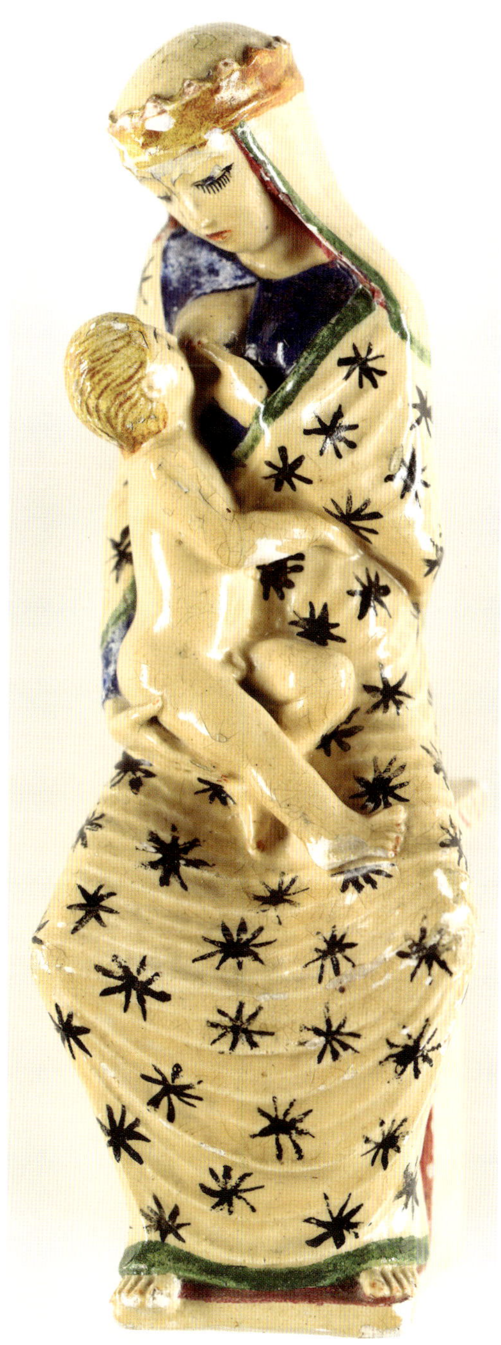

Plate 1. Madonna by Eric Gill, painted by Desmond Chute *c.*1919.

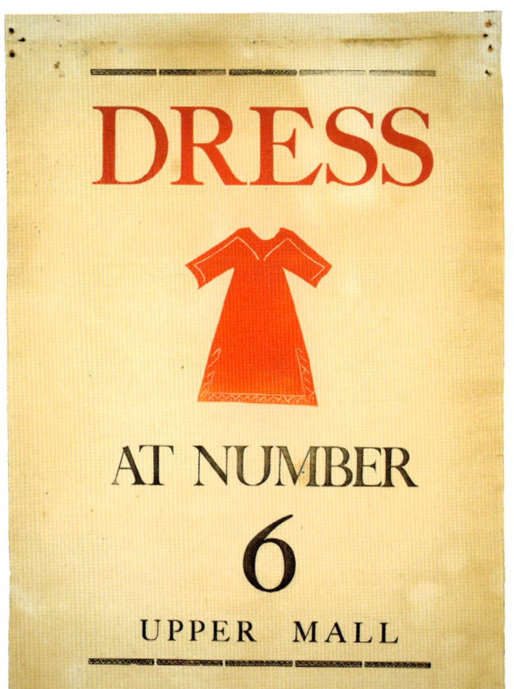

Plate 2. Hampshire House Workshop. Wood engraving, 1915.

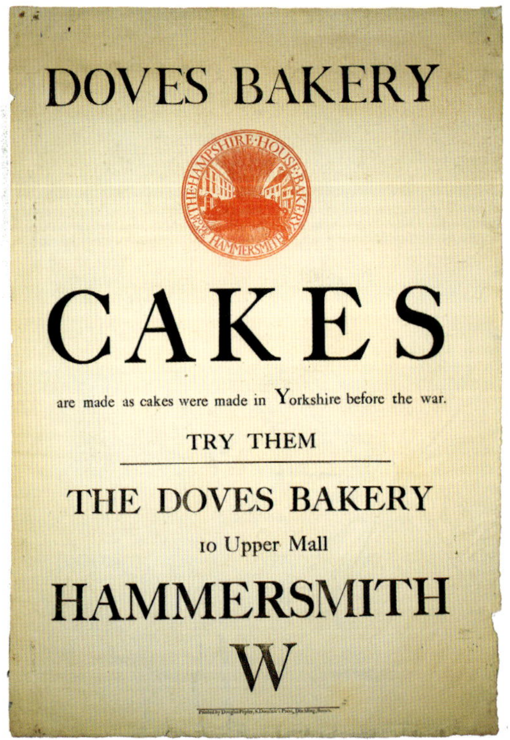

Plate 3. Doves Bakery. St Dominic's Press. Wood engraving, 1916.

Religious Questions

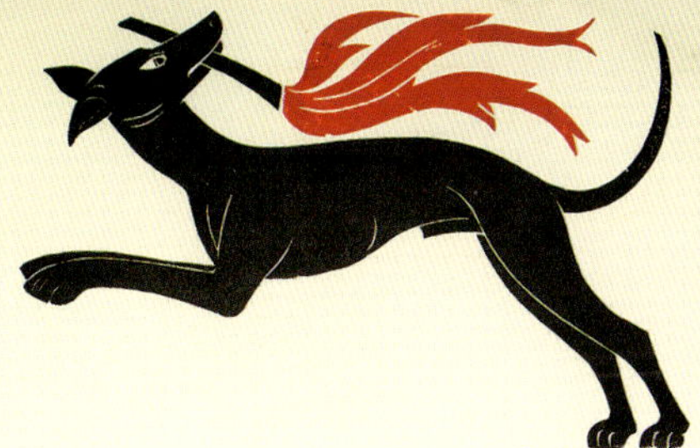

LECTURES

BY DOMINICAN FRIARS

Fr. Hugh Pope, O.P., S.T.L., D.S.S.

Fr. Hilary Carpenter, O.P.

The Nature and Existence of God.   The Immortality of the Soul.

Are Miracles Possible?   Reason and Faith.

The Meaning of Conscience.   Is Prayer a Real Force?

Growth in Faith.

Sun. Jan. 27th to Fri. Feb. 1st at 8.30p.m.

Sunday 3rd at 11a.m.

Guildhall, Cambridge.

Questions invited after each Lecture

Plate 4. St Dominic's Press, includes Eric Gill's engraving of the hound of St. Dominic, 1923.

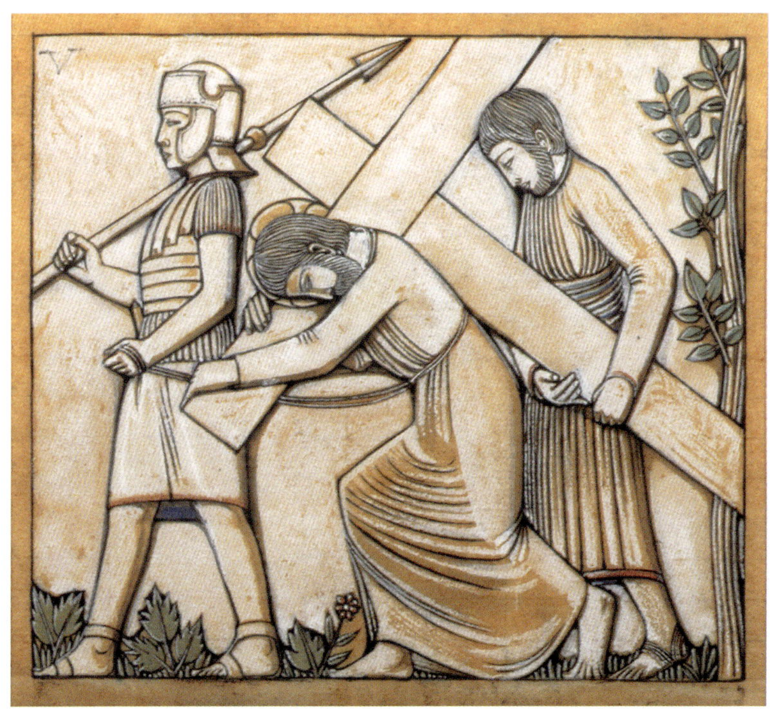

Plate 5. Fifth Station of the Cross. Gill's second drawing for a trial panel to be submitted to the Westminster Cathedral authorities for approval.

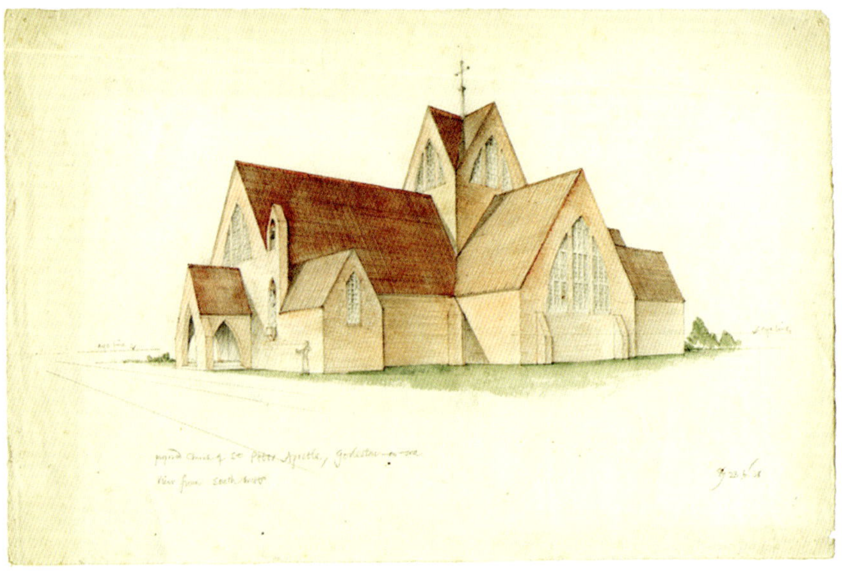

Plate 6. Eric Gill's watercolour sketch of St Peter's, Gorleston-on-Sea.

sculpture on new BBC building'.[4] Despite another visit from Mr Goldsmith, who came with Mr and Mrs Solomon 'from [the] BBC' in December 1929,[5] there followed a break of nearly a year before the next visit. The process was brought to an end after the October 1930 exhibition when the BBC appointed two Board members, Mr Goldsmith and Dr Rendall, to finalise the content and choose the sculptor, overriding Solomon and Myer. One of the first actions they took was to visit Gill on 13 November 1930; Gill did not meet with Myer until 9 December 1930,[6] and correspondence shows that both Myer and Solomon were unhappy with the BBC's unilateral actions.[7]

By the end of 1930 Gill had been appointed as the only sculptor for the relief panels and the main figures, at an initial estimate of £1,600.[8] Gill's appointment sparked debate and his association with Jacob Epstein and the decoration of the London Underground headquarters was presented as problematic. Violet Duchess of Rutland wrote to the *Morning Post* to object to Gill's appointment, referring to the 'malformations at St James's Park Station'.[9] Val Myer defended the pieces, saying:

> it is with my enthusiastic approval that to Mr Eric Gill has been entrusted the task of producing the panels and groups in which are to be concentrated the rich decoration and interest which will enhance and be enhanced by the simplicity of my own work.[10]

On seeing the images shared with the newspaper, however, the Duchess was quoted as saying 'it is awful… All I can say in its favour is that it might have been worse, and that it is better than the work with which Mr Epstein and Mr Henry Moore generally favour us.'[11] Myer's defence of Gill is important for both his own success and that of Gill's: Myer had chosen the site and size of each of

---

4   Clark Library, UCLA. Eric Gill Diary, 30 Oct. 1929. [CL]

5   CL. Eric Gill Diary, 8 Dec. 1929.

6   CL. Eric Gill Diary, entries 13 Nov. & 9 Dec. 1929.

7   This was also a financial problem for Myer and Solomon, and they were eventually able to pay Smith, Wheeler, Jagger and Lambert a nominal sum for their work up to that point.

8   A team of designers and architects also worked on the interior decoration of the building lead by Raymond McGrath, including Serge Chermayeff, Wells Coates, Dorothy Warren-Trotter and Edward Maufe. This seems to have been organised at the same time, and from early 1931 the level of correspondence regarding the decoration reduces considerably.

9   BBC WA. Book 9A. Violet Rutland, 'London's Public Statuary', letter to the *Morning Post*, 29 May 1931.

10   BBC WA. Book 9A. Col. Val Myer, 'Modern Cult in Sculpture, Mr Eric Gill's Work, Architect's Reply to Criticism,' letter to the *Morning Post*, 29 May 1931.

11   BBC WA. Book 9A. Violet Rutland, 'Modern Cult in Sculpture, Mr Eric Gill's Work, Architect's Reply to Criticism,' *the Morning Post*, 29 May 1931.

the sculptures in designing the exterior of the building and needed Gill's sculptures to be in harmony with his vision; Gill needed the continued support of his patron as well as to understand Myer's vision and so create these harmonious sculptures. Later R.R. Tatlock, writing in the *Daily Telegraph* in March 1933 described Gill's work as 'utterly different' to Epstein's *Morning* (for the London Underground headquarters), though the two might be compared: 'Epstein is a coarse and insensitive carver but an extraordinarily good modeller. Gill, on the other hand, is at his best, as here, when he is cutting into hard Portland stone.'[12]

In October 1930, just prior to Gill's official appointment to the project, Rendall set out his, and the BBC's, plan for the decorative scheme which, with one slight variation, became the final sculptures produced by Gill. Rendall's plan was as follows:

> I now put forward my own suggestions, which rest upon the personality of Shakespeare's Ariel, the poetic embodiment of Aerial. They are to some extent pictorial; but much great sculpture has been of this order. On the other hand, I have endeavoured to keep them simple in character, and everything is significant.
>
> *A.* The Central Niche
> *Prospero*, standing or seated, *delivers the pan-pipes to Ariel*, a boy child of about thirteen or fourteen years of age – Ariel might be kneeling before him, but I expect the artist would prefer that both should look outwards. Prospero would, I imagine, be fully gowned and bearded; Ariel nude, unless he carried a fawn-like skin or something similar across his body. This might make a very dignified and charming group. Ariel alone would look a bit disconsolate.
>
> *B.* The Three Panels
> 1. *Ariel is borne up by two winged angelic figures.* This idea is taken from the charming figure of Mary of Anjou similarly supported (on her tomb at Naples). The conception is of Ariel learning celestial harmonies. It fills the space admirably.
> 2. *Ariel stands piping to a circle of children.* This may portray the message of wireless to children, or, if the whole company are piping (as I prefer), it may include other ideas involved in the development of broadcasting.
> 3. *Ariel*, with his pipes slung over his shoulder, *stands between* two severe figures, *Justice and Wisdom*, who hold out their emblems, the balance and … the compasses.
>
> All these conceptions are fully sculpturesque. It is my own strong desire that we should depart as far as possible from the work of Epstein and his imitators. I hope an artist will be chosen who is capable of scrupulous and beautiful work.[13]

12 BBC WA. Book 9A. R. R. Tatlock, 'Something Rich and Strange, Fortunate Medium,' *Daily Telegraph*, 15 March 1933.
13 BBC WA. S167/4/5. Dr. Rendall, MSS, early Oct. 1930.

The subject matter was confirmed, therefore, at the time of Gill's appointment, and Solomon and the BBC took a close interest in the development of the designs. Solomon requested that Gill show him the sketches and for him to understand that 'the sketches must have my approval before Gill proceeds to completion'.[14] The extant drawings for the relief panels are in two sets,[15] and each set presents two different designs: the initial drawings for all three panels, dated 10 February 1931, depict full-size figures within the rectangular space. They are quite detailed, and the figures have lithe bodies and flowing wavy hair. Four days later, on 14 February 1931, Gill produced another series of drawings. The drawings for the three reliefs change from detailed and stylised to increasingly abstract and simplified. Between these two sets of drawings Gill visited the BBC to see the site for the carvings – a trip that could have changed his view of the current designs. He may also have seen his patrons, possibly taking the drawings with him, and then incorporated their feedback. During the trip Gill visited an Epstein exhibition at the Leicester Galleries where he would have seen a number of bronze portraits as well as the large marble *Genesis* carving, completed by Epstein the year before. Following the approval of the drawings, Gill carved models in stone before he and his assistants started work *in situ*.

Gill's work on the BBC sculptures, in particular on *Prospero and Ariel* (Fig. 15), was followed closely by the printed media from early 1931 until the unveiling in 1933. According to Fiona MacCarthy it was with his work for the BBC that Gill firmly established his reputation, and when he became known as an eccentric and given the nickname 'married monk'.[16] It is clear from the newspaper articles dating from this period that Gill's physical appearance became as important as the work he was carrying out. The *Evening News* in July 1932 wrote of seeing the 'remarkable head and shoulders of Mr Eric Gill, bearded and bereted (or is it an old-fashioned skull cap this modern sculptor wears?)' appear over the top of the canvas behind which he was working *in situ* on *The Sower*:

> Mr Gill wears a smock and two pairs of spectacles at his work, and is altogether an unusual figure. His beard is black, he has piercing, dark eyes, and he looks as if he had strayed from a Montmartre *atelier*, where his studio is an enormous barn at his charming place at High Wycombe in Buckinghamshire.[17]

A photograph illustrated this article, the caption for which read 'Mr Eric Gill,

---

14   BBC WA. S167/4/5. Robert Solomon to George Val Myer, 8 Jan. 1931.

15   These drawings are in the William Andrews Clark Memorial Library and in the archive of the Monotype Corporation in London.

16   Fiona MacCarthy, *Eric Gill* (London, 1989), p. 247. MacCarthy does not provide the reference for this quote.

17   BBC WA. Box 9A. 'What's Behind the Screen'? *Evening News*, 7 July 1932.

in his beret and clogs, at work in his studio'.[18] The majority of articles on Gill's work for the BBC appeared around the time of the unveiling of *Prospero and Ariel* in early 1933. The *Evening News*, echoing its earlier article, visited Gill on 1 February 1933 on the scaffold erected around the piece *in situ* and described him as 'a strange bearded figure girt with something that might have been a trench coat, shod in rubber shoes, and crowned with the honourable remains of a once black beret'.[19] The article was illustrated with the same image of Gill that had appeared the previous year – of him carving in his Buckinghamshire workshop.

In the *Daily Telegraph* the physical nature of the work was described, with emphasis being placed on Gill's hardiness in completing the work:

> Mr Gill has climbed 25 feet up a ladder four or five times a day for four months to work on these figures, his only protection from wind, rain and snow being a narrow sheet of glass suspended just above Prospero's head.[20]

The *Manchester Guardian* in an article entitled 'Furniture Pieces at the BBC' stated that the sculptures had been viewed by 'a small party active enough to climb a long ladder',[21] thus emphasising the physicality of the process of carving the sculptures. The article then described Gill's appearance: 'Mr. Gill [was] wearing a blue beret and picturesque muffler and clothes, his brown beard trimmed to a more Renaissance shape than it used to be'.[22] Gill was described as a 'master carver'[23] who had worked for four months in all weathers on the scaffold to finish the piece. The *Manchester Guardian* explained that the quote 'furniture pieces' came from Gill himself:

> Where did art come in? 'Oh, art,' said the sculptor, 'is skill. Don't let's talk about art. It's like the dentist's work, stopping teeth, and the carving here has made much the same kind of noise. Prospero is a symbolic piece rather like the three balls over a pawn–broker's shop.' He denied that it was sculpture. Sculpture was something that was part of the building, not mere ornament. 'Prospero' and 'The Sower' were ordered by the owners for decoration.[24]

From the above quotes it is possible to assert that Gill saw the panels as forming part of the building and so they were not sculpture; *Prospero and Ariel* and *The Sower* on the other hand were disconnected and therefore more akin to decoration

---

18   *Ibid.*

19   BBC WA. Box 9A. 'A peep at Ariel and Prospero', *Evening News*, 1 Feb.1933.

20   BBC WA. Box 9A. 'BBC 'Prospero' Finished, Mr Gill's view of his sculpture, 'Furniture Pieces', *Daily Telegraph*, 15 March 1933.

21   '"Furniture Pieces" at the BBC', *Manchester Guardian*, 15 March 1933.

22   *Ibid.*

23   *Ibid.*

24   *Ibid.*

and sculpture than to architecture. On the day of the unveiling of *Prospero and Ariel* to the press an article by Gill was published in *The Listener* in which he analysed the characters; he wrote that the

> stone carving is to be regarded as heraldic rather than architectural sculpture. It is only a work of art in a low sense of the word…This carving is meant to be a useful object. As walking sticks are useful to lame men, so this carving is intended to be useful to the passer-by – useful as a sign and a symbol, like a cross on a tombstone or the three balls on the shop of a money-lender.[25]

Gill here used his existing ideas on the importance of a coherent connection between architecture and sculpture to explain the appropriateness of his work and thereby explain his place within the commission. At the same time, however, he distanced himself from the content of the work by associating himself with the role of a contractor under orders.

One local MP called for the sculptures, in particular *Prospero and Ariel*, to be removed on the grounds of decency; Gill's response indicates his view of his own responsibility towards the subject matter. The *Evening News* interviewed Gill in March 1933, in which he justified Ariel being naked by saying that the BBC specifically requested it:

> I suppose I ought to feel offended, and talk about art with a big A, but it is just too absurd. After all, why blame me, in any case? Even if I had deliberately carved an indecent statue, the BBC would not have put it up, and' – he spoke confidentially, with a trace of pride – '*they liked Ariel*'.[26]

Gill, in this article and elsewhere, presents himself as following the orders of his client and creating what was requested of him. Two trains of thought were presented by him in the press: that of the loyal contractor creating what was requested of him with little personal responsibility; and that of an artist needing to explain his appointment as a contractor by explaining the 'heraldic' meaning of the finished works.

Later in 1933 Gill was again interviewed in the *Manchester Guardian*. In 'Artist and Patron' he clearly stated his views on patronage and the artist's role. The interview was featured in a short piece earlier in the newspaper, which summarised Gill as preferring 'to have his instructions and to have them precise'.[27] Gill's problem, as presented in the article, was that too often the patron's instructions were not precise enough because patrons did not always know what they

---

25 Eric Gill, 'A Sign and a Symbol', *The Listener*, 15 March 1933, p. 397.
26 BBC WA. Box 9A. *Evening News*, 23 March 1933, 'Those BBC Statues, By the Man Who Made Them'.
27 *MG*. 'Artist and Patron', 23 Sept. 1933.

wanted; the result was that they left the artist to himself and then complained about the result. The newspaper stated it was in broad agreement with Gill's points: 'Mr. Gill's distinction between the "art of the studio" and the art of the portrait or public monument is rightly made.'[28]

The full interview on a later page is revealing not only with regard to Gill's approach to working with architects, but also to what appears to be an openness in discussing in detail his working methods.[29] The article presented Gill's sculpture for the outside of the newly built choir-school for Manchester Cathedral:

> Mr Gill started work on the relief at his home by getting one of his apprentices to do the preliminary cutting away of stone from the rectangular block. Apprentices must learn their trade, he explained, and they must start with something they cannot spoil.[30]

On being asked by a passing member of the public if he was carving in a Byzantine style (as had been asked about his Westminster Cathedral *Stations of the Cross*), Gill told the newspaper: 'I have none of the tricks of an architectural carver with centuries of tradition behind him … In a kind of way I am almost an amateur.'[31] This brings in another aspect into Gill's view of himself and his work: the humble 'amateur' craftsman working within a medieval tradition of guilds, apprentices and journeymen completing work to order.

In the articles discussed above, Gill seemed to be interested in distancing himself from the concept and meaning of the work during and after completion. In his statements Gill concentrated on the symbolic nature of the sculpture as heraldic, in particular *Prospero and Ariel*. He was concerned about the appropriateness of the subject matter on that particular building: by comparing it to the pawnbroker's three balls he was saying that the sculpture should be a signifier for the broadcasting function of the building. Gill's public and private statements on the meaning of the sculptures suggest that he wanted to distance himself from his patrons, and place the responsibility for the commission with them. In a letter to his brother, written halfway through completing the work, he wrote of 'the BBC kidding itself that it may be likened to a sort of wise old prince putting the world to rights and its bally apparatus likened to a sort of heavenly sprite!'[32] In an interview with the *Evening News* on 1 February 1933 – six weeks before the sculptures were unveiled – Gill admitted to the journalist that he wondered 'what the public will think of them … Some will say it is Marconi

28 *Ibid.*
29 Cf. below, Chapter Six, for further discussion on the point.
30 *MG* 23 September 1933.
31 *Ibid.*
32 Walter Shewring, (ed.), *Letters of Eric Gill* (London, 1947), p. 267.

– some Father Christmas. But there you are, it is none of my business.'[33]

Gill's idea that it was 'none of [his] business' what the sculptures depicted or symbolised implies a view of himself as an artist-contractor, hierarchically beneath his patrons in questions of content and intention. Archival material relating to the making of the sculptures provides a narrative of Gill's approach, as well as a useful context within which to examine the meaning of the sculptures and Gill's public views of his commission. Photographs taken by Howard Coster, a well-known photographer of artists, reveal Gill's working process on the models, each of which were done at a third the size of the final piece. The practical process of carving the sculptures took place in both the workshop and *in situ*. The stone for the panels was already in place when Gill started work; his workshop assisted him in carving out the top layers which he then finished. The panels were finished mid-1932 and Gill then started working on the large Prospero and Ariel *in situ*. The work for this piece had also started in the workshop, with the majority of the roughing out work done by his assistant, Lawrence Cribb. Gill started carving the large stone for *Prospero and Ariel* on 8 January 1932.

Gill made two models for the figures of *Prospero and Ariel*; (Fig. 16) the first one was not used and was later re-carved and re-named by Gill as *Abraham and Isaac*.[34] The second version became the model for, and is almost identical to, the full-size carving at the BBC. The differences between the two are minimal but significant: in *Abraham and Isaac* the figure of Isaac is taller (relative to Abraham) than the figure of Ariel (relative to Prospero) in the second model; Abraham appears more passive with a longer flowing beard and hair and what seem to be closed eyes; Isaac also stands on the top of a globe whereas the model of Ariel stands on a flat ground. The globe on which Isaac stands is referred to in Rendall's original scheme proposed in October 1930:'There is a sphere at the base on which the figure might stand; this, however need not be retained.'[35]

In order for the piece to become *Abraham and Isaac* Gill removed the pipes and depicted Isaac's hand in the gesture of blessing. This was done between 1933 and 1936. (Fig. 17). In a letter to *The Listener* in 1936 Gill described how he came to abandon the first model:

33   BBC WA. Book 9A. *Evening News*, 1 Feb. 1933,'A peep at Ariel and Prospero'.

34   In Gill's diary both models are referred to as *Prospero and Ariel*, and Collins's catalogue records that the one that became *Abraham and Isaac* was the second model made by Gill 'for his own pleasure'. Judith Collins, *Eric Gill The Sculpture: A Catalogue Raisonné* (London, 1998), p. 204. However, photographs in the archive at the University of Notre Dame show the almost finished *Abraham and Isaac* version in the background of the *Prospero and Ariel* model half-finished, indicating that in fact *Abraham and Isaac* was started first and then abandoned as the model.

35   BBC WA. S167/4/5. Dr Rendall undated MSS early Oct. 1930.

> in the course of carving it I came to the conclusion that the proportions of the
> figures to one another were not appropriate to the subject, so I abandoned it…
> If anybody chooses to compare the two groups he will see that the sizes of the
> figures in relation to one another are quite different and that…in the Prospero
> and Ariel the relation is that of magician to fairy (i.e. the figure of Prospero is
> monstrous and that of Ariel much smaller than any natural child could be in
> relation to a parent).[36]

In this letter to *The Listener* Gill presented a realisation during the making of the
model that he had created an image that did not fit the purpose of the subject
matter requested; it also evidences a close interaction between artist and patron
as well as Gill's engagement with the meaning and purpose of the group. During
his work on the first model Gill was visited by Myer and Rendall at his workshop
in April 1931, and Coster took photographs of it on 6 May which were probably
sent to other stakeholders. Gill did not begin carving the second model until
20 May, indicating that though it may have been a decision made by him, his
patrons were likely to have had some involvement either in person or by seeing
photographs.

At some point between finishing the second *Prospero and Ariel* model in
1932, the unveiling of the full-size group at the BBC in early 1933, and the sale
of the model to the Tate (through the Leicester Galleries) in 1935, Gill carved
stigmata on the figure of Ariel. It is unlikely that this was a feature of the model
when it was inspected by the BBC, the architect and the syndicate. In the letter
quoted above to *The Listener*, Gill also expressed a view he later repeated in his
Autobiography:

> In my view the figures at Broadcasting House are as much God the Father
> and God the Son as they are Shakespeare's characters, and so it is quite appro-
> priate that the group at the French Gallery should be either Joseph and Jesus or
> Abraham and Isaac, for all these things are different views of the same thing.[37]

In his *Autobiography* Gill wrote of the commission: 'I took it upon me to portray
God the Father and God the Son. For even if that were not Shakespeare's meaning
it ought to be the BBC's.'[38] He presented the scheme as a failure:

> I mean simply that I don't much like looking at them. The idea was grand but I
> was incapable of carrying it out adequately. Prospero and Ariel! Well, you think.
> *The Tempest* and romance and Shakespeare and all that stuff. Very clever of the
> BBC to hit on that idea, Ariel and aerial, Ha! Ha! And the BBC kidding itself,

36   Shewring, *op. cit.*, pp. 369–70.
37   Ibid.
38   Eric Gill, *Autobiography* (London, 1940), p. 249.

in the approved manner of all big organizations (British or foreign, public or private), that it represents all that is good and noble and disinterested.[39]

Gill's complaint, in looking back at this commission, was that the symbolism of *Prospero and Ariel* was stretched too far by the BBC and so he was not able to fulfil their requirements. This attitude reflected an ambivalence that was in evidence in the 'Artist and Patron' interview: that it was the patron's responsibility to be clear on the intention of the piece in order for the sculpture to have clarity in meaning. It also allowed Gill to publicly dissociate himself as 'author' of the pieces, instead becoming the 'maker' – the hands, to the head of the BBC.

Subsequent historical narratives of Gill's commission repeat the idea, stated by Gill in 1936 and in his *Autobiography*, that he had planned to carve *Prospero and Ariel* as God the Father and God the Son from when he first received the commission. At the time, however, Gill publicly stated that as the sculptor he was following the instructions of his patrons and the piece could have any meaning: the most important of these meanings was in the hopeful apprehension in the sculpture of the function of the building. Gill's alteration of the models enabled him to give them a religious meaning. His actions (carving the stigmata on the second model, changing the title of the first model to *Abraham and Isaac*, and his public statements) have subsequently influenced historical interpretations of the full-size group at the BBC as being an intentionally religious sculpture. Gill's use of the image of *The Sower* and *Ariel* in engravings he was making in the early 1930s for the Golden Cockerel Press's *Four Gospels* also emphasise this interpretation.

In Gill's writings on architecture he was in search of unity between architect, worker and sculptor. In this he referred to his co-translated version of Jacques Maritain's *Art et Scholastique* (1920), in particular the identification of the artist (or architect) with the work being produced:

> To the work to be done, that it may turn out well, there must answer in the soul of the workman a disposition which creates between the one and the other that sort of conformity and inmost proportion which the schoolmen call 'connaturality'.[40]

Connaturality, meaning innate, or of the same nature, is presented as the basis for the connection between the artist and beautiful and meaningful work to be produced. Gill's ideas take this further by stating that this connection must exist between all workers and their product, and, importantly for sculpture and building, between the architect and the artist. This collaborative approach to the

---

39 *Ibid.*, pp. 248–9.
40 Jacques Maritain, *The Philosophy of Art*, trans. Rev. John O'Connor and Eric Gill (St Dominic's Press, 1923), p. 14.

work renders problematical not only the idea of a sole author of a particular work or building, but also the relative importance of the artist alongside the architect.

Gill's role within his workshop was that of the master; in his architectural commissions he saw himself taking the role of contractor reporting to the master architect and the patron; at the same time he aimed to form a close working relationship that ensured harmony in thought between the two. The importance of this relationship, for Gill, was central to the success of the work as a signifier of the function and form of the building, and some of his public statements indicate that he often did not reach this harmonious way of working. Gill's own statements, in which he can be seen to distance himself from the intentions of his clients, are challenged by his subsequent deliberate attempts to assert his own responsibility for the works by changing the meanings and selling them as stand-alone Gill sculptures. The final version has subsequently become both a symbolic, secular, statue made in collaboration with the BBC architect, syndicate and board of Governors, and a religious sculpture by Gill.

Eric Gill in Manchester   6

M. J. Broadley

Eric had no particular love for a city which had given its name to the gospel of industrial capitalism.[1]

… in terse epigrammatic sentences [Gill] *destroyed almost the whole of Manchester.*[2]

Eric Gill's preferred self-description and chosen epitaph was that of *stone-carver*; Manchester has few mementos of him in that capacity. Of Gill the letter-cutter, there are but three memorial inscriptions; in subject, location and date order these are as follows: Francis Thompson, University of Manchester (1912); John Trego Gill (uncle of EG), Manchester Crematorium (1912); George Gissing, University of Manchester (1913). As stone-carver, there is only one example: a relief in Stancliffe stone depicting the four figures of St Mary trampling a dragon, the Christ Child, St Denys and St George, above the door of the former choir-school of Manchester Cathedral. (Fig. 18). A proposed war memorial in Portland stone for the church of the Holy Name was never executed; the only evidence of it is a drawing, signed by Gill, held at the Courtauld Institute, London.[3] (Fig. 19). An instruction on the drawing reads: 'please return to Eric Gill, Ditchling Common, Sx'; in the bottom right-hand corner appears what is presumably the date of the drawing: 24.5.[192]2.

Gill left his mark on Manchester, the first industrial city, more in opinions fashioned in the spoken word, hewn from his notions of industrial society and belief in social justice, rather than by stone-carving or letter-cutting. This chapter

---

1 Robert Speaight, *The Life of Eric Gill* (London, 1966), p. 234.

2 *Manchester Evening Chronicle*, 8 September 1933. In an interview Gill gave for that paper he claimed that 'the Town Hall is just mad' due to the fact of its having been built in the Gothic style, thus it was incongruous with Manchester, a nineteenth-century city.

3 David Peace, *Eric Gill The Inscriptions* (London, 1994), mentions an 'Inscription for a figure in Hopton-Wood stone, painted in black, blue and red: Iesu, Iesu, Iesu, Esto Mihi Iesus. Done in collaboration with Desmond Chute.' p. 91. (Dated 12 September 1918. The same inscription is seen on the proposed memorial for the Holy Name, Manchester (cf Fig. 19). The phrase may be taken to mean: *Jesus, Jesus, Jesus, be to me a Jesus* (= Saviour); it is taken from the *Jesus Psalter*.

will look first at what he had to say in relation to the Cathedral carving, and then examine a lecture he gave to the Link Society entitled 'Money and Morals', where he expressed ideas on economics and what he called the 'machine-age'; these could not have been more antithetical to those of the 'Manchester School'.

The Salford Diocesan Archives hold two items relating to 'Money and Morals'.[4] The first is a photograph of Gill standing next to Bishop Henshaw, the fifth Bishop of Salford, on the evening of the lecture. (Fig. 20). The second is a postcard, in Gill's own hand, requesting that if entry to the lecture was by ticket only, then one be sent to a Miss May Reeves, at Garstang. (Fig. 21). Gill stayed with her when working on the Manchester Cathedral sculpture. The simplicity and commonplace nature of these items belie their significance as evidence both of the event they record and, more obliquely, of other more labyrinthine matters.

During the time he was engaged with the Cathedral commission, September to November 1933, Gill spoke on subjects so fundamental to him they might rightly be said to have defined who and what he was: the art of stone-carving; a loathing of industrialism; and an impassioned concern for social justice. He spoke of the first in an interview for the *Manchester Guardian* entitled 'Artist and Patron', in which he discussed the Cathedral commission.[5] Using this as illustrative of his general view on the sculptor's craft, he explained his own method of working. Initial work on the carving was begun by an apprentice in Gill's workshop; he believed that apprentices, when learning their trade, 'must start with something they cannot spoil'.[6] Later work was done *in situ*, thus allowing Gill to see the work under the conditions of light in which the finished article would be seen by the passer-by. As for the panel itself, he had simply been asked to provide figures of the Cathedral's patron saints. The Dean and Canons had offered no further instructions, having accepted Gill's sketch of the relief without comment. He did not know whether the Dean and Canons wanted a pictorial scene of saints adoring the Madonna and Child, or – as Gill presumed – 'three hieratic figures'. The way the figures were to be carved was dependent upon what was required and the way they were to be depicted. Gill would clearly have preferred more detailed instruction: 'if a patron commissions a mahogany table with four legs and rounded corners to seat ten people he gives you a definite artistic problem. If he merely commissions a table you do not know where you are or what he

4   Salford Diocesan Archives, SDA 480.

5   *Manchester Guardian*, 23 Sept. 1933.

6   David Kindersley, a one-time apprentice of Gill, remembered how 'mistakes always had to remain … He believed that most mistakes resulted from a lack of attention and encouraged us to concentrate on what we had conceived in our minds.' David Kindersley, *Mr Eric Gill Recollections of David Kindersley* (Ward Ritchie Press, 1967), p. 9.

wants.[7] He spoke of having had a similar experience when carving the Stations of the Cross for Westminster Cathedral. In that instance he had been given clear instructions for only one of the fourteen Stations; the rest he had to decide for himself as to what figures to show and how this should be done. The reason why a sculptor was not given directives he traced to 'the artistic tyranny of the last few centuries, the product of the Renaissance'. This had given rise to the idea, now firmly fixed in the mind of the general public, that 'the artist was a seer who was not to be interfered with'. Gill thought it to be entirely nonsense as it bestowed on the artist a duty that was not rightly his. Gill considered the artist's duty to be that of the contractor, and so at the service of the patron.[8]

As to the discussing of sculpture, Gill believed there were two ways in which this might be done. The first sprang from the artist's original intention; the second, from what critics might discover in the finished work. Of the latter approach, an example was to be seen in how the depiction of the Christ Child in the Cathedral panel drew favourable comments as being appropriate for its position over the doorway of a school. Although this was not part of his original intention Gill felt able to concur with it as a valid interpretation.

The interview allows a further glimpse into how Gill envisaged the nature of sculpture. It was, he thought, 'more a process of deciding to leave things than of deciding to do things'. For example, he decided that the dragon – depicted under Mary's feet – ought to have a tongue, so he left sufficient stone for this purpose. He went on to explain how 'it so happened that the dragon's tongue touched St Denys' toe. Should I leave it so? The dragon, conquered by St George, is fitly placed under Our Lady's foot as an offering. It is also tamed that it licks the bishop's foot, and so I decided to leave it.'

A passer-by is reputed to have asked if the carving was in the Byzantine style; Gill replied that he did not know. During the interview he enlarged on this, saying how 'in a sense it was so', given that he lacked 'the tricks of an architectural carver with centuries of tradition behind him', elaborating further: 'in a kind of way I am almost an amateur … I am back in the Saxon, or primitive period, in one sense, not through design (*sic*) to do primitive carving but because this is the way in which carving must begin.'[9] Curiously, Gill's later autobiography contains a similar comment, made when he was working on the Westminster Stations: 'they thought I was carving in the Byzantine style … Certainly I was carving in what might be called an archaic manner.'[10] Whether both stories are true or

---

7   *MG*. 23 Sept. 1933.

8   The at times complex nature of the relationship that existed between Gill and his patrons is further explored above by Ruth Cribb in *Chapter Five*.

9   *MG*. 23 Sept. 1933.

10   Eric Gill, *Autobiography* (London, 1941), p. 200.

apocryphal, the point remains: in recounting them Gill wanted to communicate *his* way of doing things, and how *he* thought carving should be. As a stone-carver he chose not to copy from a clay model, preferring to draw the outline of the design on to the stone and then carve directly. David Kindersley, one of his former apprentices, remembered how Gill 'thought and then he made his thought in stone'.[11] The first time he employed this method – the carving of a figure of a young woman in stone – he describes thus:

> So all without knowing it I was making a little revolution. I was uniting what should never have been separated: the artist a man of imagination and the artist as workman … I really was like the child who said 'first I think and then I draw my think' … Of course the art critics didn't believe it … They thought I was just putting up a stunt – being archaic on purpose. Whereas the real and complete truth was that I was completely ignorant … and was childishly doing my upmost to copy accurately in stone what I saw in my head.[12]

Bearing this in mind, and with reference to the Cathedral sculpture, one might say that Gill departed Manchester having left his thoughts behind – carved in stone above the choir-school door.

The lecture which he gave shortly after completing the Cathedral relief provided him with the opportunity to air his views on those other topics which were so characteristic of him: antipathy to industrialism and concern for social justice. On that occasion however, rather than simply airing views he chose to sow the wind; the whirlwind he would reap when the lecture was published. Briefly, his primary thesis was to the effect that under the present economic system the practice of Christian morals was for most people extremely difficult, if not almost impossible. A secondary thesis being: Catholic priests were complicit by their silence in not condemning strongly enough a corrupt economic system.

'Money and Morals' is of particular significance in the development of Gill's ideas. Robert Speaight reckoned it 'introduces the Eric Gill of the later years with what can only be described as a bang'.[13] It is a Gill who is didactic, angry and impatient. The lecture took place under the auspices of a Salford diocesan organisation known as the Link Society. The aim of the society was the furthering of Catholic Action; membership consisted, although not entirely, of former university students. There is no clue as to why this particular subject was chosen. Certainly Gill was left free to choose his own title; it remains within the realms of possibility that he took the opportunity to speak his mind about all that Manchester

---

11   Kindersley, *op. cit.,* p. 21.
12   Gill, *Autobiography*, p. 162.
13   Speaight, *op. cit.,* p. 235.

represented in the history of industrialism and economics.[14] Fr John O'Connor from Bradford, Gill's friend and confidant, was present and proposed the vote of thanks. Speaight writes: 'the bishop took the chair for the lecture, wondering – rather understandably – what he was in for.'[15] The lecture was first published in abbreviated form in *The Colosseum* (June 1934), the full text followed in *Money and Morals* (1934). What was the bishop in for? To that we must now turn.

Gill began writing the lecture on 19 October 1933,[16] continued working on it for the next two days and delivered it on the evening of 15 November 1933 at the Holdsworth Hall, Manchester. He took the title of the lecture from a letter of the bishop: '"Money and morals! Personally, I have not much of the former, but the latter cause me a great amount of trouble."'[17] This encapsulated for Gill 'in one sentence the whole situation today. We have not much money – but morals cause us a great amount of trouble.'[18] He proposed therefore to show during the course of the lecture that an intimate connection existed between the two – a connection which, judging by his comments, the bishop had seemingly failed to make. But who was he, 'a mere stone-carver and letter-cutter', to speak about money when on the subject of monetary theory he was a layman, asked Gill?[19] He reassured his listeners that it was precisely in the terms of a layman, rather than as a monetarist, that he would address them. The same would go for morals: he would not speak as a moralist; his concern was not with sin or with the health of people's souls, but with what people do.

His first step was to dispel the commonly held notion that money was in limited supply.[20] This myth was perpetuated by the Bank of England controlling the issue of currency. However, currency consisted of two forms. The first, *notes and coins,* is minted by the Bank of England; the second, *credit,* is controlled not by the Bank of England but by private banks. The myth arose from affixing on the first form and forgetting the second; its falsity proven by private banks creating credit to an

14 On an earlier occasion, having been asked to address a group of Catholic students at Manchester University on the subject of the relation of sculpture to architecture, he thought 'it was rather an important occasion . . . and [I] took it as a good opportunity to work up a statement'. Cf . Walter Shewring, (ed.), *Letters of Eric Gill*, (London, 1947), p. 217.

15 Speaight, *op. cit.*, p. 235.

16 The published text appeared in *Money and Morals* (London, 1934). The MSS of the lecture is dated 19 October 1933; this strongly suggests that the text Gill used in the lecture and the later published version were, apart from some possible editing, largely the same.

17 Eric Gill, *Money and Morals* (London, 1934), p. 1.

18 *Ibid.*, p. 1.

19 *Ibid.*, p. 2.

20 It is perhaps worth bearing in mind whilst Gill was speaking of the shortage of money in terms of it being a 'myth', the country as a whole was experiencing the height of the Depression. I am grateful to John Hogdson for this insight.

amount equalling ten times more than was available in notes and coins. Effectively this amounted to making money out of nothing, and was akin to God creating *ex nihilo*. For Gill this demonstrated how powerful and god-like the banks were. Lending the money they create and charging interest on the loan was 'obviously the most gigantic system of usury the world has ever seen'.[21] Gill poignantly observed how Shylock lent only from the money he actually had in his bag, whereas banks lend what they do not possess. The creating of money by private banks represented an important public service, and ought therefore to be under the control of the Treasury and Parliament. He believed that if this were so there would be no need for any other form of taxation.[22] The self-effacing, self-confessed non-specialist in monetary matters is now playing the role of advisor to the Treasury.

Gill rejected the prevailing view of money as a trading commodity to be bought and sold – as happens in the city and by the banks, and juxtaposing it with the Christian practice of alms-giving, he concluded: 'far from being economically unsound, it is the soundest possible economic policy'.[23] Giving money to a beggar demonstrates precisely the proper use of money; for it is given to him to spend, not to invest. Being neither good nor evil, money possesses of itself no value. Gill defined it as nothing more than 'a commonly and publicly accepted standard of exchange. 'E.g ... this pencil is worth fourpence.'[24] In other words it was a flux, enabling the flow of things to the consumer. In an industrial society money proved necessary because we are unable to produce all that we need and some things we must therefore purchase. Despite these contrary views, Gill made it clear he was not advocating a return to a pre-industrial age:

> Can we return to a simple undeveloped state? Does anyone want to? A few people want to – but very few. It seems necessary to assume that a general return to a society of self-supporters, with a system of barter ... for such exchanges as cannot be avoided, is neither possible nor desired.[25]

Gill had now clarified the nature, purpose and function of money; he next turned the attention of his audience to the subject of morals. He had already explained at the start of his lecture that sin and the health of people's souls were not his concern; he would speak of morals in terms of what people *do*.

In order to demonstrate the nexus between money and morals Gill carefully laid down the initial tenet of his argument: 'the first thing to be remembered

21 Gill, *Money and Morals*, p. 9.
22 In a footnote he writes: 'I have this on the authority of the reported words of Mr. Hawtrey, financial adviser to H.M. Treasury.' *Ibid.*, p. 8.
23 *Ibid.*, p. 9.
24 *Ibid.*, p. 10.
25 *Ibid.*, p. 11.

is that in morals as in faith there is a necessary natural basis.'[26] Revealed truth presupposes natural truth, and revealed morals presuppose natural morals. Faith fulfils the human mind and Christian morals fulfil the will and natural appetites. They do not add anything extraneous to human nature; they lead rather to nature's perfection. Before one can believe as a Christian one necessarily has to have a certain way of thinking: 'the ordinary laws of thought must be accepted.'[27] Gill explained . . .how it logically followed that certain ways of thinking were incompatible with Christian faith; for example, Kantian Idealism. Thus far he had not said anything new nor extraordinary. Extrapolating from this principle he posited the same for natural morals. Since they are connatural to mankind it follows that certain ways of living were incapable of being a preamble for Christian morals: for example, slavery. Given that both free will and responsibility are fundamental to Christianity, a slave deprived of these cannot act responsibly. Gill gathers the strands of his argument into a leitmotif: 'a state in which human responsibility is denied or underdeveloped or diminished is a state in which Christianity is denied or underdeveloped or diminished.'[28]

The next movement in this orchestrated assault on industrialism is to demonstrate how this was applicable to industrial Britain. Gill considered factory workers to be enslaved, unable to exercise freely the responsibility belonging to them as human beings; 'the factory hand is not responsible for what results from his obedience' to the factory owner.[29] Industrialism had deprived them of responsibility, whereas Christianity demands responsibility. He was willing to accept that there may well be individual Christian workmen, but theirs would be a diminished kind of Christianity:

> For men are men all the time and not only in their spare time – the time when they are not at work – and a state in which men are fully responsible. . .only when they are not working. . .is a state in which Christianity and the Christian notion of human responsibility are undeveloped or diminished.[30]

He concludes: 'a state founded upon what we call the factory system or industrialism is a state founded upon a way of living and working definitely incompatible with Christian morals.'[31]

Having spoken of the necessity of certain preambles for Christian belief and morals, and having shown how some ways of living are incompatible with both,

---

26 *Ibid.*, p. 15.
27 *Ibid.*, p. 16.
28 *Ibid.*, p. 18.
29 *Ibid.*, p. 20.
30 *Ibid.*, p. 20.
31 *Ibid.*, pp. 18–19.

Gill had positioned himself for a devastating attack on industrialism and the machine-age. He carried through his attack with what Speaight described as 'the naïveté of his unrelenting logic':[32] the present economic system was so radically corrupt that it was well-nigh impossible to practise moral virtue. Taking several aspects of contemporary economics, he illustrated why this was so.

What was it that rendered industrial society so inimical to the flourishing of Christianity? The fundamental fault with industrialism Gill identified as its provision of 'unlimited goods for consumption', yet 'of its own nature' it provided no education for consumers.[33] In point of fact, industrial production was destructive of education; quoting words of Fr Martin D'Arcy SJ: '[the] methods of production "reduce the worker … to a subhuman condition of intellectual irresponsibility"'.[34] Good mechanics and good machine-minders were without doubt being turned out, but they were not responsible for what they did or what they made. Gill considered them to be no more than uneducated 'morons, cretins, semi-imbeciles', whose highest form of amusement are 'cross-word puzzles, slimming, football competitions, watered beer, sham half-timbered bungalows, Burns and Oates church statues'.[35] Gill had illustrated his ideal of the workman's responsibility during his interview with the *Manchester Guardian*, where he spoke of apprentices being given sufficient space that allowed for mistakes to be made. However, once made they were not to be corrected – the apprentice must become responsible for what he makes and does.[36] Such caustic remarks about factory-workers justify one in thinking that his ideas about work were set at too high a level and so beyond the reach of the 'ordinary workman', they were in fact as unrealistic as they were idealistic.

The problem as Gill saw it was that the workman, the consumer, was not educated in the right manner. In an industrial civilisation education is considered 'as a thing for spare time – a thing to keep people happy when they are not working – to keep them out of mischief.'[37] An educated workforce was of little profit and of no use to industrialists who needed factory hands, 'cannon fodder', rather than people with initiative. In such a context, education is nothing more

32   Speaight, *op. cit.*, p. 70.

33   Gill, *Money and Morals*, p. 21.

34   *Ibid.*, p. 21. Gill often quoted these words of D'Arcy so that they become almost a personal mantra for him.

35   Gill, *Money and Morals*, p. 22.

36   During interviewing for 'Portrait of Eric Gill' former apprentices recalled how Gill instilled in them the importance of being 'true to the medium'. They were never allowed 'to fake anything, mistakes had to remain. We redesigned if there was a mistake.' There was never 'any question of patching up.' Cf. www.bbc.co.uk/archive/sculptors.

37   *Ibid.*, p. 22.

than an opiate, an instilling of a sense of obedience – 'Not theirs to reason why'. Under such conditions Gill asserts that Christianity cannot flourish.

Economic circumstances were no less prohibitive: the state when 'people cannot buy what they need, even though they, by their combined labour, may have made what they need, is a state in which Christianity is denied or undeveloped or diminished'.[38] Quoting St Thomas Aquinas, Gill drives home the implications: 'a starving man needs food not instruction'.[39] Paradoxically, the expectation is for the proletariat to receive a high level of instruction, but only grudgingly is enough food provided to keep them alive. This is corrosive of society, for when 'men are compelled by the circumstances of their lives to grab and grasp like starving wolves, the notions of charity and justice will diminish and disappear'.[40]

By depriving people of their responsibility and effectively enslaving them, the industrial system has reduced man to 'an animal condition of physical determinism'.[41] Gill observed how this may pass without notice in such places as Oxbridge colleges – 'where they live in the tradition of medieval good living', but it is noticeable in the slums of Manchester and in the offices of businessmen.[42] The physical environment in which people exist impacts upon their ability to live morally – this is what Gill is claiming, as he makes clear: 'a certain civilisation … is as much a necessary preamble to Christian morals as a certain mentality is the necessary preamble to Christian faith'.[43] He substantiates this claim with reference to Canon Barry of Leamington: 'Our interminable rows of tenement houses contain many men and women who are not really human, and it is folly to think of Christianizing what is not yet in any fair way of being civilised,'[44] yet little cognizance was given to this fact. Despite countless material blessings brought by industrialism, the majority of people continue to live in a state of chronic physical insecurity and anxiety which impedes Christian morality. Referring to Fr Vincent McNabb OP, Gill shifts the focus from general principles to the concrete, particular situation of daily living, signalling how: 'the economic conditions of the people make abstention from the practice of birth control a matter of heroic virtue'.[45] To expect heroic virtue is unreasonable, especially when life is becoming increasingly more difficult economically. Yet a high and unrealistic

38 *Ibid.*, p. 23.
39 *Ibid.*, p. 23.
40 *Ibid.*, p. 27.
41 *Ibid.*, p. 24.
42 *Ibid.*, p. 24.
43 *Ibid.*, p. 24.
44 *Ibid.*, p. 24.
45 *Ibid.*, p. 26.

expectation has become the norm: 'All our well-meaning organisations for the improvement of morals – Boy Scouts, Girl Guides, the Grail … are all organisations for the inculcation of virtue – virtue which has become heroic'.[46] Gill stresses that the matter is not one of 'bad people', but simply of 'bad economics … artificial scarcity in a world of plenty', the evidence for this is seen in fruit left to rot, coffee being burned and surplus fish thrown back into the sea.[47] Bad economics frustrates moral behaviour, 'being good is economically impossible'.[48]

Canon Drinkwater had already identified the crux of the matter: 'the economic problem fills the whole sky … nothing can be done, nothing, until the economic problem of money has been dealt with'.[49] To Gill's mind it was nothing less than scandalous that no notice was taken of the fact that the issue of money was monopolised by banks and that unemployment was not diagnosed as the disease that it is, but rather as a symptom of health and progress. Moreover, a blind eye was turned to the fact of the total production of the nation being in the ownership of a handful of capitalists, when in reality it belonged to the whole nation. The popes' insistence that labourers have a right to a fair share in the product of their labour prompted Gill to ask 'why do we not give a dividend to everyone as we give a pension to a retired colonel?'[50] In reality, the prevailing economic and industrial environment was one where wage-earning was viewed merely as a contract between employer and employee, between the buyer and the seller. The present situation was a direct consequence of the policy of earlier generations, when instead of giving workers a share in the profits, the wealth created was invested to gain yet more.

Gill believed that the entire system was simply mad – an attempt 'to run an imbecile system'.[51] Citing the words of Jacques Maritain, 'the first need of our time is an intellectual need,'[52] Gill made a plea for intellectual clarity in order to counter the toxic nature of contemporary, industrial society. The ones who should provide this clarity – the clergy, the spiritual leaders – were failing to do so. Gill thought the majority were 'in the position of men standing on the brink of a frozen pool and shouting to men drowning under the ice that they should take good deep breaths if they want to be healthy'.[53] Yet for him the answer was an obvious one:

46   *Ibid.*, p. 27.
47   *Ibid.*, p. 26.
48   *Ibid.*, p. 27.
49   *Ibid.*, p. 40.
50   *Ibid.*, p. 29.
51   *Ibid.*, p. 36.
52   *Ibid.*, p. 36.
53   *Ibid.*, p. 36.

> There would be no sex problem, no marriage problem, no prostitution problem,
> no birth control problem, no population problem, no unemployment problem
> if our economic problem were solved. Is the economic problem insoluble? Is
> rational finance impossible?[54]

In reply to these last two questions Gill suggested the following, for which he made no claim of infallibility. Of paramount importance was the abolition of the trade in money, especially its international trade. The focus of the financial system should be moved away from bankers and moneylenders and placed on consumers – the people who use money. The Government ought to regulate the supply of currency so that purchasing power is equal to productive power. That it be acknowledged that the total production of a nation belongs to all the people, not just to the capitalists; this would abolish the distinction between capitalist and proletarian. Gill considered the proletariat to be a legal fiction: 'there is no such thing as a proletariat – a person who owns nothing but his labour power. England and all that is in it belongs to the English'.[55] To speak of private property as a natural right is really to say, 'private possession is a natural right … private use is a natural right'.[56] Finally, we must recognise that the best thing to do with savings is to spend them, and to stop insisting on our being usurers by investing and lending money.

The nature of the main problem remained crystal clear in his mind: it was an economic one, and economics were at the heart of many moral problems, particularly those concerned with population and birth control.

'No doubt there will always be wicked men; but who knows how much legal crime – theft, drunkenness, swindling, chicanery and meanness of all sorts is caused by the frantic absurdity of a world in which, while every necessity is to be had in plenty, enormous numbers of people are short of food, clothing and shelter, and the majority of the people live in the fear that to-morrow they will be thrown on the scrap heap'?[57]

Gill had made clear the enslaving and destructive effects of industrialism and capitalism: restricting the flourishing of Christianity, and by an intolerable burden frustrating the practice of virtue. He had made no less clear his own solutions to the economic problem – and this despite his protestations at the beginning of the lecture that he was a layman in matters of finance.

He began to assemble his second thesis: that the clergy were, by remaining silent and thus failing to condemn the economic system, implicitly culpable

54 *Ibid.*, p. 36.
55 *Ibid.*, p. 39.
56 *Ibid.*, p. 39.
57 *Ibid.*, p. 41.

in the moral dilemma that he had identified. Gill's criticism is sharp: 'it seems clear that the clergy are barking up the wrong tree when from the altar steps they talk about sin to people who have been deprived of the possibility of living according to common natural morals.'[58] In order to make Christian morals possible he thought it vital that people have first the necessities of a human existence, only then could morals be taught. Yet instead of doing something to resolve the economic situation, 'moralists fulminate against the selfishness of modern young people'.[59] This led him to make a most controversial conclusion: until the economic problem was addressed and the financial system altered 'the teaching of Christian morality … is a waste of time.'[60]

The much needed intellectual clarity was available, and readily so, in *Rerum Novarum* and *Quadragesimo Anno*, the social encyclicals of Popes Leo XIII and Pius XI, respectively. Both stated that a resolution to the economic problem *is a matter of the Kingdom of God and its justice*. Gill described as 'a happy hiding ground' that attitude whereby engaging with social justice was avoided by the claim that Christ's Kingdom 'is not of this world'.[61] Papal teaching asserted that whatever deprives man of what is natural to him cannot be of God. Gill asks rhetorically: 'has the Church no concern with Society or with politics, social reform; no use for money; nothing to say about usury; nothing to say about working conditions? If this is the case, he asks, why were these encyclicals written? If Christ was not concerned with the weary and overburdened why did he feed the four thousand, why did he have compassion on the multitude?[62]

Gill begins to conclude by asking, 'What then is to be done? What is the best politics for our time?'[63] Not naïve to the fact that no modern nation is going to banish machinery, and that its use was likely to increase, he remained insistent that the machine age, the 'beehive state', was incompatible with human nature and so ultimately doomed to failure. Nonetheless, the beehive state appeared to be what most people wanted and no one was trying to prevent it; the likelihood was that the future would be likewise. Therefore a *modus vivendi* had to be adopted as an interim policy. Gill's suggestion of Communism as the only just and natural alternative political system must have caused some stir amongst the audience. His reasons for doing so were based on his belief that the wide use of machinery necessarily creates large enterprises; inevitably these will assume the nature of public services. He gave the example of how 'the railways are public

58   *Ibid.*, p. 46.
59   *Ibid.*, p. 28.
60   *Ibid.*, p. 41.
61   *Ibid.*, p. 48.
62   *Ibid.*, p. 48.
63   *Ibid.*, p. 48.

services however much their dividends are owned privately.'[64] It seemed logical that when a worker was providing a public service then that service should be publicly owned. Gill reminded his hearers – perhaps to placate them – that such ownership was essentially the idea of Communism; he sweetened the pill by adding how it was, moreover, 'analogous to a return to the Feudal System' where all property is held in trust, this system was not at odds with Church teaching.[65] In this scheme of things the first public service to pass into public ownership would be the issuing of currency; its remaining in the hands of private companies was something that 'cannot be tolerated'.[66] Those who control this service have command of the whole nation; alluding to *Quadragesimo Anno* Gill protests of:

> a despotic economic domination … by those who hold and control money – who because they hold and control money are able to govern credit and determine its allotment, for that reason supplying, so to speak, the life blood of the entire economic body, and grasping, as it were, in their hands the very soul of production, so that no one dare breathe against their will.[67]

He was 'not advocating Communism as a desirable form of state organization in itself'.[68] In his autobiography Gill would describe it as much 'an equally bloody tyranny' as capitalism.[69] The alternative would be Fascism – state ownership favoured by big industrialists. Faced with such an option Gill is all for Communism as the only just politics. In his opinion the concepts of justice and love did not exist in the minds of big industrialists, given that the nature of business is by definition to make money. In the beehive state there seems more likelihood of justice if ownership is vested in the proletariat as a working man rather than in men of business.

And what role is there for the Church in the beehive state? It will, as always, stand in the position of the poor relation, the leaven in the lump. Gill ends with the clarion call:

> We can no longer escape responsibility … Red and purple – medievalism – incense, gothic architecture, all the ritual business! Would it not be better to weed out all these things? For one person they attract there must be a hundred they repel – repel, because they are bad heraldry – they do not proclaim the real thing …The medieval supremacy of the Church has not survived.We are back in the catacombs – whether we like it or not.'[70]

64 *Ibid.*, p. 51.
65 *Ibid.*, p. 52.
66 *Ibid.*, p. 52.
67 *Ibid.*, pp. 52–3.
68 *Ibid.*, p. 53.
69 Gill, *Autobiography*, p. 281.
70 Gill, *Money and Morals*, p. 59.

Lest anyone might have missed the nub of his lecture he made a final attempt to sear it on the memories of his audience: 'We have to make it clear that a certain way of living is the necessary preamble to Christian morals'.[71]

What effect did the lecture have? Evidence is lacking as to what the audience made of it or how it was received. Gill made no comment on it in his diaries; the press, Catholic and secular, failed to report it. A delayed reaction occurred in the wake of the lecture's subsequent publication. Speaight again: 'a small book might be written on the disagreement provoked by *Money and Morals* among those who were Eric's closest allies'.[72] The abbreviated text in *The Colosseum* confined itself to repeating the premise of the second part of the lecture: 'no man can live according to the precepts of Christian morals unless a certain way of living and general laws of life be both possible and practised'.[73] To illustrate this, Gill had added examples taken from the Ten Commandments. Criticism of the Catholic clergy maintaining silence in the face of economic injustices remained forthright. Canon Barry and Frs D'Arcy and McNabb were, in their denunciations, 'rare flutes'; the 'rest of the orchestra is silent'. Gill asked, 'is it notorious that [the Church] is against the commercial world and all its usury? It is not … only the big trumpet speaks and he is far away in Rome'.[74] He ends the article by saying, 'The point is that the life of the people is filched from them and still the clergy {only} talk about our sins'.[75]

Michael De La Bedoyère's critique in the *Catholic Herald* comments on the courage it took to speak out: 'Mr Gill is shouting, and not without reason'.[76] In a subsequent issue of the same weekly Fr John Baptist Reeves OP, took the opposing view. He was the brother of the May Reeves for whom Gill had requested a ticket for his lecture; at the time she was also Gill's mistress and a future model for his *Twenty-Five Nudes*. Fr Reeves took Gill to task – 'shouting was not the Catholic way of doing things', as it only resulted in making virtue more difficult.[77] This was not the only fault identified by Reeves; he commented: 'in the statements lately quoted from him here, and in many others publicly

---

71 *Ibid.*, p. 59.

72 Speaight, *op. cit.*, p. 239. Speaight quotes letters from Tom Burns and Louis Bussell, written to Gill in response to *Money and Morals*. Burns disagreed with Gill's 'clean sweepism' (pp. 40–2); Bussell failed to see how machines were the cause of the loss of responsibility (p. 243).

73 Archives of the British Province of the Society of Jesus, 40/4/3 'Morals and Money' [*sic*]. This quotation is taken from an off-print entitled 'Morals and Money' [*sic*]; the script has been corrected in a few places. The file, marked 'Martin D'Arcy materials', contains numerous appraisals and type-scripts.

74 Archives of the British Province of the Society of Jesus, 40/4/3.

75 *Ibid.* { } denotes correction to original script.

76 *Catholic Herald*, 16 June 1934.

77 *CH.*, 30 June 1934.

made by him on similar topics, there is not yet the full measure of Christian prudence, or justice, or temperance.' With regard to this lack of virtue, Reeves awaited the opportunity to, as he put it, 'break a lance with Mr Eric Gill', albeit in a light-hearted manner.[78]

With the appearance of *Money and Morals* in its entirety Reeves, taken aback at the things Gill had said, wasted neither time nor effort in seizing the opportunity 'to very seriously challenge the whole treatise of the essay'.[79] Furthermore, the issue was too serious to reply with the levity he would have much preferred.[80] In summarising Gill's argument he seemingly twists what *Money and Morals* claims about the clergy; by doing so he accuses Gill of something that he never said nor implied: 'the Catholic clergy are largely, if not wholly, to blame for the economic conditions which make Christian morality impossible'. Reeves further misrepresents Gill when he accuses him of 'insisting that the moral fault for [the] moral defects' of the laity lay with the clergy. Reeves, in his own words: 'very seriously challenge[s] the whole treatise of … *Money and Morals*', both its primary thesis: 'that Christian morality is exceedingly difficult, if not impossible, under existing economic conditions'; and 'much more [the] secondary thesis: that the moral responsibility for the general moral failures of Christian morals rests with the Catholic clergy.'[81] As for the statement on which Gill built his argument – 'Christian morality presupposes natural morality, just as Christian faith presupposes a natural apprehension of truth' – he takes no issues; the truth of which 'is patent to any well-trained mind'.[82] Gill, in wrongly interpreting the principle, had rendered it false; as a result the conclusions he drew 'are demonstrably false … opposed to facts and contradicted by reason'.

78 *CH.*, 10 Nov. 1934.

79 *Ibid.*

80 The question is raised as to whether Reeves was aware, or suspected, the nature of the relationship existing between his sister and Gill at the time; if so, did this explain partly the severity of his reply? Such a question is a tantalising one; for did anyone outside of the immediate circle of Gill's family know about his sexual compulsions? In a radio programme, 'Eric Gill, My Brother', featuring Cecil Gill, the latter said: 'Eric and his family lived in great simplicity, and in an aura of shockingly free thought. I suspected free love and all kinds of licentiousness. How wrong I was I only know now.' BBC Written Archives, 'Eric Gill, My Brother', by Dr Cecil Gill, 20 March 1951. Philip Hagreen, a one-time member of the Guild of St Dominic was also seemingly oblivious; after having reading Speaight's biography of Gill, noted: 'Much of what had to be told came as a shock to me … I remonstrated when I thought he was doing harm, but he was beyond the range of any gun. There must have been some mental kink that allowed Eric to be humbly devout when he was behaving outrageously.' Lottie Hoare, *Philip Hagreen: A Sceptic and a Craftsman*, p. 7. Available at www3.nd.edu./~jsherman/ Hagreen

81 *CH.*, 10 Nov. 1934.

82 *Ibid.*

Reeves's refutation rests on the intrinsic nature of the relationship between nature and grace. Grace is not a substance; it is an accident, and must therefore inhere in a substantial nature that is *essentially* perfect. If that nature was, or were to become, radically corrupt then it cannot and could not coexist with it. It was on this point that Gill had erred, for he had assumed that 'before grace can exist in a man or an angel that man or angel must be already *naturally* perfect.'[83] Reeves drew the distinction of how nature need not be naturally perfect in order to be receptive to grace. In summary, Reeves notes: '*when grace is in any nature* that nature must be essentially, though not necessarily in every respect, an essentially perfect nature.' This is what is meant when St Thomas speaks of 'grace perfecting nature'. A nature which is radically corrupt cannot correct or perfect itself, no more than a dead body can reanimate itself. The cause of perfection is grace assisting nature, not the efforts of nature alone.

Reeves illustrates the above by the example of Christ calling 'not the righteous but sinners' to perfection: 'morally the Pharisees were eminently respectable and the system of economics under which they lived would have given Mr Gill very little reason for complaint', yet it was the publicans 'whose morals were awful and whose economic practices were even worse' who were won over to perfection.[84] It is in what Reeves describes as, the 'soil of a sinful and corrupt society' where grace works; and when it does, traces of corruption may well remain.

The *coup de grâce* to Gill's argument is administered with Reeves's judgement that: 'Mr. Gill's thesis is only true if sin and economic disorder are synonymous.'[85] At the beginning of his lecture Gill recognised how, 'an immoral life may not be a sinful life.'[86] Taking this latter claim – that sin is not synonymous with immorality – Reeves asserts that it would be illogical to claim that grace cannot co-exist with economic disorder. If the economic system is not sinful then it is not 'a radical corruption of human nature';[87] it is not naturally perfect, but neither is it totally corrupt. As for the priests: their duty is to preach the Gospel and administer the Sacraments. An economic system is only their concern as priests if and when it is sinful; and it 'must be ascertained whose sin it is, for sin is a personal, not a social, evil'. The reforming of the economic order begins therefore with individual conversion, or as Reeves put it: 'let Mr. Gill and you and me go and show ourselves to the priest'.

---

83   *Ibid.*
84   *Ibid.*
85   *CH.*, 10 November 1934.
86   Gill, *Money and Morals*, p. 1.
87   *CH.*, 10 Nov. 1934.

Ever eager to argue and debate, Gill replied to Reeves's comments in a letter to the Editor of the *Catholic Herald*. His opening phrase has the air of condemning with faint praise: 'a lot of what he says is rather over my head and, therefore, runs like water off a duck's back and, so to say, cuts no ice'.[88] The divergent view taken by his critic Gill attributes to the fact that he may possibly have misled him by failing to present a clear and coherent argument. He therefore clarifies his position with the summary example of how a starving man is, according to Church teaching, allowed to steal bread in order to survive. In such cases theft is not stealing. Offering further clarification he writes: 'if the natural requirements of physical life are withheld our judgement of people must be different from what it would be if they were prosperous'.[89] Gill points out that the matter is not quite so simple in the case of the industrial system, however; as this is the cause of unemployment, enslaves human beings, destroys the family, creates competitive markets and involves war.

Gill acquits himself of having accused 'the Catholic clergy of being largely to blame for the institution of industrialism', by claiming that all he did was to 'complain' that only rarely do priests realise 'that the industrial system is inimical to Christianity', and that 'the clergy rarely preach against avarice.' The only justification for such silence would be if the Church is to be 'the little flock' and if Christian virtue was always to be heroic virtue. Gill raises the objection that this is not the line taken by the papal encyclicals, and that Christ had compassion on the multitude. Likewise with the necessities of life, all he is claiming is that in the absence of food, clothing and shelter 'few people will either care for salvation or listen to preachers.' He recognises that the clergy do indeed have compassion on the multitude. As a corrective to their silence he asks for 'it to be notorious, that the Church is as much the enemy of injustice as she is the friend of the righteous.'[90] Gill wants it to be seen to be disproved that the Church is silent because 'she has too much money invested in the industrial system.' He ends his reply with a postscript: 'I say nothing about "Nature and Grace". Of course, I accept, without demur, what the Church teaches about that.'

With this he demurs from entering into a theological debate. He was not a trained theologian, nor had he read systematically the works of St Thomas Aquinas.[91] What theology he did possess was gleaned from Dominicans such

---

88 *CH.*, 1 Dec. 1934, cf. Shewring, *op. cit.*, pp. 314–7.

89 *Ibid.*

90 *Ibid.*

91 Cf. Rene Hague's comments made during the interview 'Portrait of Gill", first broadcast 20 June 1961, available at www.bbc.co.uk/archive/sculptors. Gill mentions in his diaries reading St Thomas's *Summa* on 9 and 16 February, 2 and 9 March 1913. He was received into the Catholic

as Vincent McNabb and Austin Barker and members of the Third Order of St Dominic, among them Canon John Gray, Dr Patrick Flood, and of course by the reading and discussing of Jacques Maritain's *Art et Scholastique*; this debt he acknowledges in his autobiography.[92] The exaggerated claims of *Money and Morals* remained therefore unsubstantiated. He also failed to define what constitutes 'a certain way of living'; as Donald Attwater has pointed out: 'Gill was looking at a very high and enlightened and unrestricted standard of life and conduct.'[93] Fr Martin D'Arcy SJ, in the 1961 BBC radio programme 'Portrait of Eric Gill' described him as having a marvellous philosophy of life; at the same time this was accompanied with a misconception of man. This manifested itself in *Money and Morals*. D'Arcy believed that 'Eric belonged to a form of Protestantism which said that in the face of money you were practically incapable of being good.'[94] He spoke also of how Gill, 'fell into the fallacy of perfectionism: the present condition is an unfortunate one, round the corner is the true condition of human life'. Gill had not resolved the issue which John Baptist Reeves had identified: the relation between nature and grace.

If, as Speaight conjectured, a small book might have been written about the disagreements provoked by *Money and Morals*, one could equally be written about sin and virtue, nature and grace *vis-à-vis* Eric Gill; especially post-Fiona MacCarthy's biography.[95] Until those issues are adequately addressed in relation to him it is unlikely that a more positive study of Gill's attitude to the problem of work and social justice will, or indeed can, be made. Gill thought of himself as the archetypal craftsman who made in order to use, not to sell.[96] He claimed that his life had been an endeavour 'to make a cell of good living'.[97] It follows then that his life was not, unlike that of the workman described in *Money and Morals*, subject 'to a subhuman condition of intellectual irresponsibility'.[98] The economic

---

Church on 22 February 1913. I am grateful to Ruth Cribb for this information. Gill's reading of Aquinas pre-1922, when he began to acquaint himself with Maritain's *Art et Scholastique* confirms Naomi Billingsley's suggestion that 'Gill has a genuine debt to the scholastic tradition earlier than commentators have often implied', cf. above, p. 38.

92   Gill, *Autobiography*, p. 207.

93   Donald Attwater, *Modern Christian Revolutionaries* (New York, 1947), p. 220.

94   www.bbc.co.uk/archive/sculptors.

95   Fiona MacCarthy, *Eric Gill* (London, 1989).

96   There was something of the businessman about Gill nevertheless; David Kindersley remembers Gill being asked to reduce the cost of the relief sculpture he had been asked to provide for a block of flats, to which Gil replied: 'Each leaf is £5, so if you do away with the whole branch that will save £25.' The reaction of the Directors of the project was: 'He is not an artist. He is a businessman.' David Kindersley, *op. cit.*, p. 14.

97   Gill, *Autobiography*, p. 282.

98   Gill, *Money and Morals*, p. 21 et seq.

conditions which dictated that the practice of virtue be tantamount to heroic did not therefore apply to Gill. Yet he failed to live a moral life – and failed precisely in that area of personal morality which he believed would benefit from the resolution of the economic problem. Whilst he might have been free from the latter, he no doubt had a sex problem. A fact he recognised by acknowledging how he was not 'a perfectly continent and virtuous person';[99] his behaviour was at times, to quote: 'Bad. Bad. Bad'.[100] He also acknowledged that a solution to the economic problem would not eradicate the possibility of sin.[101] MacCarthy has asked how could Gill be so religious, and yet so unchaste? As a result, 'his adherents do not like to ask this question'.[102] The answer to this conundrum, should there be one, will lie in that intrinsic relationship of grace and nature identified by Reeves in his reply to *Money and Morals*. E. Michael Jones reckons that the outrage caused by MacCarthy's biography, in which she disclosed the intimate – and sordid details – of Gill's diaries, was caused not so much by the sexual sins themselves but by Gill's 'willingness to repent of them after he [had] committed them'; Gill frequently went to Confession. Jones adds: 'in his sexual life, Eric Gill was a typical modern – perhaps a little more exuberant than most. In his spiritual life, however, he was a Catholic. And it is the conflict between the two that brings out the rage of the reviewers'.[103] This opinion is weakened however by its apparent failure to take sufficiently serious the gravity of incest.

Walter Shewring wrote in the preface to *Letters of Eric Gill* that Gill's philosophy was to some minds 'his most valuable contribution to the life of our time'.[104] If one can bring oneself to see beyond the issue of Gill's behaviour, does anything remain there for a contemporary audience? Pius XII is said to have commented of him 'this man has understood our encyclicals'.[105] The phrase 'the Church's best kept secrets' has often been used to describe the social teaching of papal encyclicals. This phrase had yet to be coined when Gill was advocating *Rerum Novarum* and *Quadragesimo Anno*. Since those days the teaching has developed substantially in both scope and depth, especially under the pontificate of Blessed John Paul II. It is a description Gill would surely have agreed with as it echoes his own thoughts on the failure of the clergy to trumpet its doctrine and ideas. It would be a fruitful exercise to compare and contrast his thoughts on the problem of

99   Gill, *Autobiography*, p. 193.
100   Quoted in Michael Jones, *Degenerate Moderns* (Ignatius Press, 1993), p. 12. I am indebted to Dr Anthony Dykes for alerting me to this reference.
101   Gill, *Money and Morals*, p. 36.
102   MacCarthy, *Eric Gill*, p. ix.
103   Jones, *op. cit.*, pp. 9–10.
104   Shewring, *op. cit.*, p. 8.
105   Speaight, *op. cit.*, p. 282.

work with the encyclical *Laborum Exercens*, written on the ninetieth anniversary of *Rerum Novarum* and in which Pope John Paul II, speaking of the 'Gospel of Work', identifies the dignity of human work, and the tensions, conflicts and crises which surround it and also tackles the problem of the 'machine age':

> While it may seem that in the industrial process it is the machine that "works" and man merely supervises it, making it function and keeping it going in various ways, it is also true that for this very reason industrial development provides grounds for reproposing in new ways the question of work … even in the age of ever more mechanized "work", *the proper subject of work continues to be man.*[106]

The role of the Church in the beehive state Gill envisaged being like that of leaven: 'a thing more or less secretly and on the quiet producing a ferment … which will eventually … disintegrate the whole inhuman thing'.[107] Pope Benedict XVI has often alluded to Arnold Toynbee's phrase of 'creative minorities' in relation to the Church in the contemporary world, where the traditional Christian culture has broken down. It is a perennial problem for the Church: living in a disapora-like situation it must not succumb to becoming ghettoised, whilst at the same time the surrounding milieu perceives it as a stranger. Here there is scope for comparison with Gill's vision of the Church being the leaven of society. In *Money and Morals* Gill, in line with various popes, sees the resolution of the economic problem as a matter of the Kingdom of God. Later developments in Catholic social teaching echo these sentiments; the 1971 Synod of Bishops spoke of:

> action on behalf of justice and participation in the transformation of the world fully appears to us as a constitutive dimension of the preaching of the gospel or, in other words, of the Church's mission for the redemption of the human race and its liberation from every oppressive situation.[108]

The above references to official documents are meant not as an oblique rehabilitation of Gill; they are merely pointers for possible further investigation. Any study of his ideas on work and its nature, and on social justice must take into account sin and virtue, nature and grace, and particularly how these were present and absent in his own life, both public and private. Whatever validity exists in those ideas remains, for as St Thomas Aquinas says, 'the truth is true wherever it is to be found'.

---

106 *Laborum Exercens*, para. 5.
107 Gill, *Money and Morals*, p. 58.
108 Quoted in Charles M. Murphy, *Theological Studies* no. 44 (1983), p. 298ff.

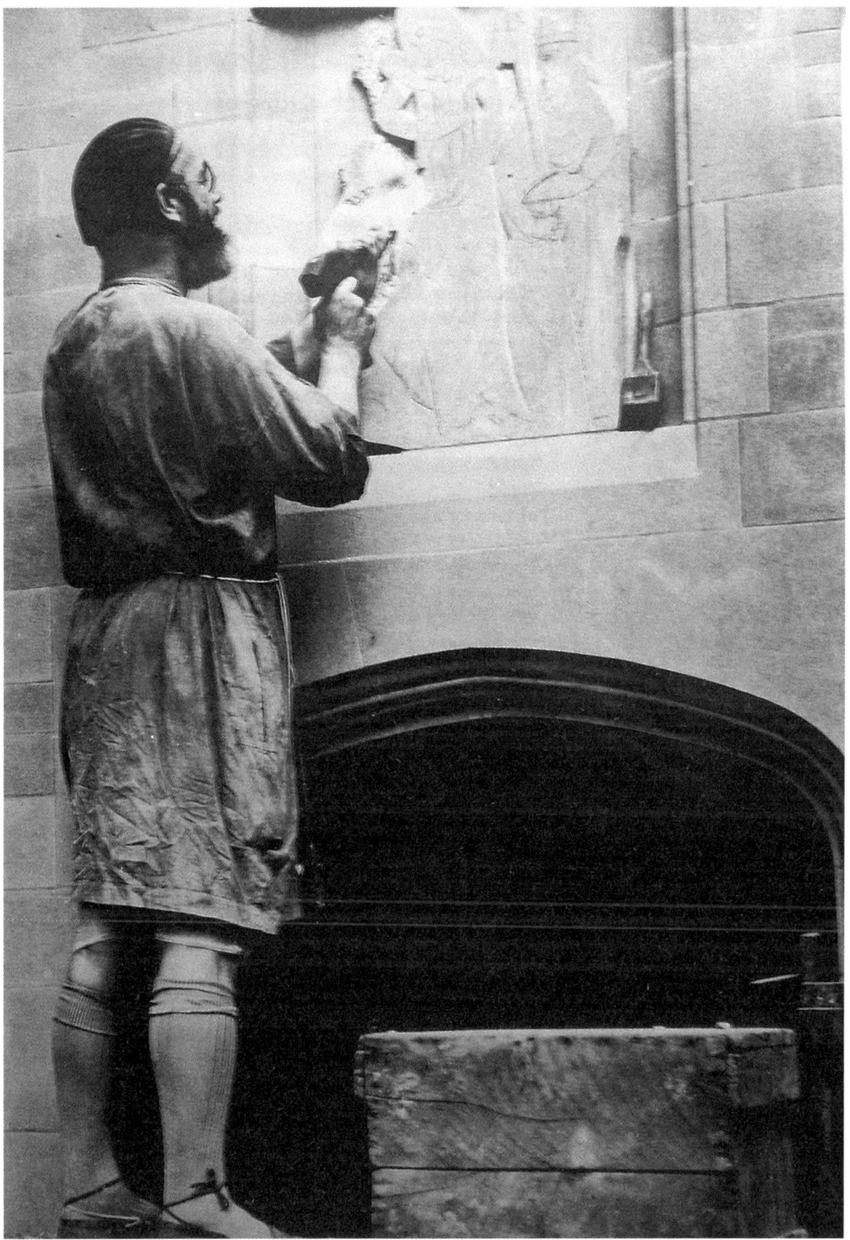

Fig. 18. Eric Gill working on the Manchester Cathedral relief.

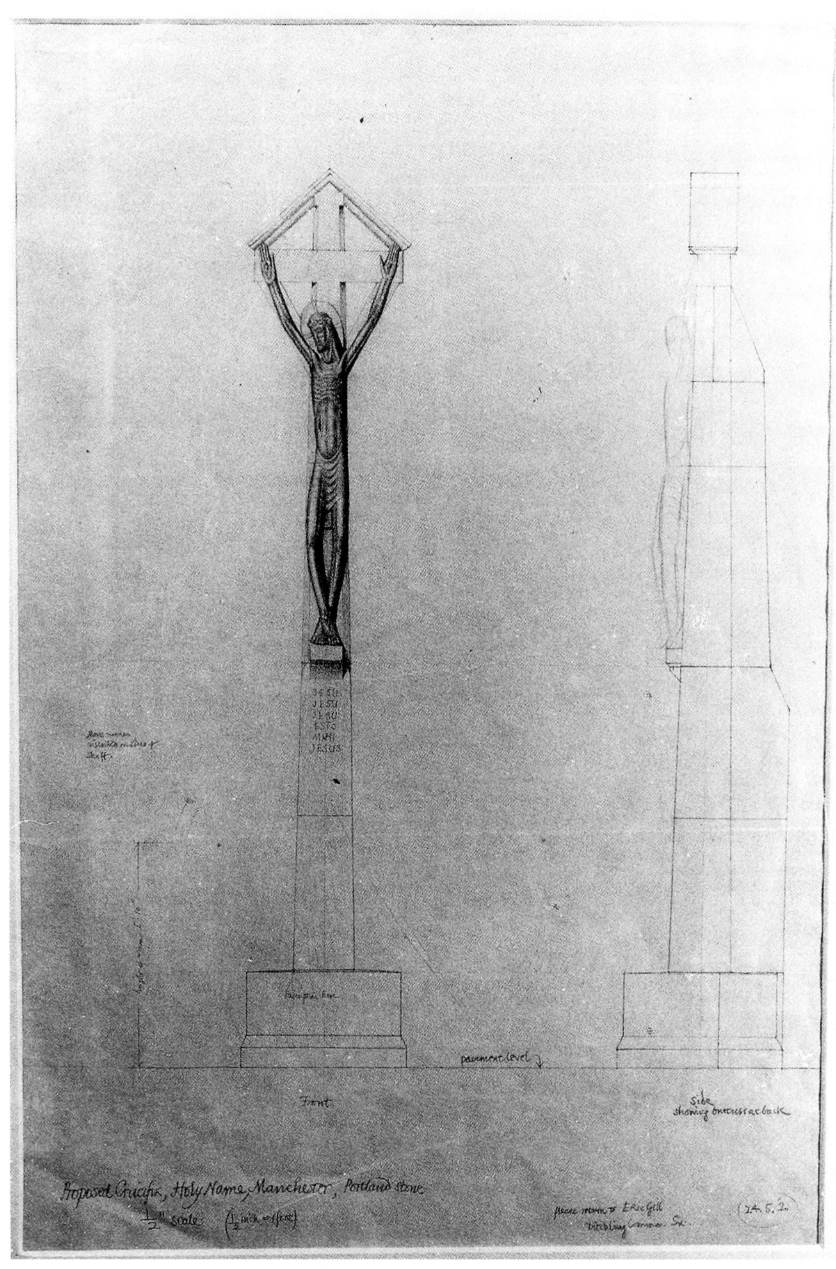

Fig. 19. Drawing of proposed war memorial for the Holy Name church, Manchester.

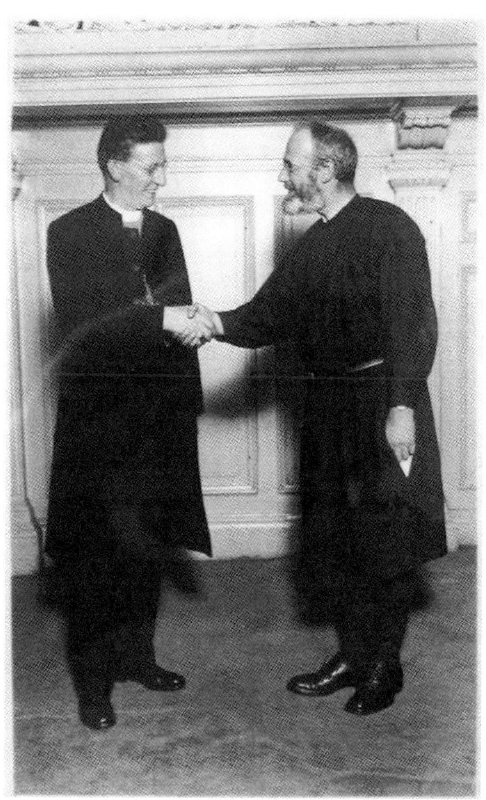

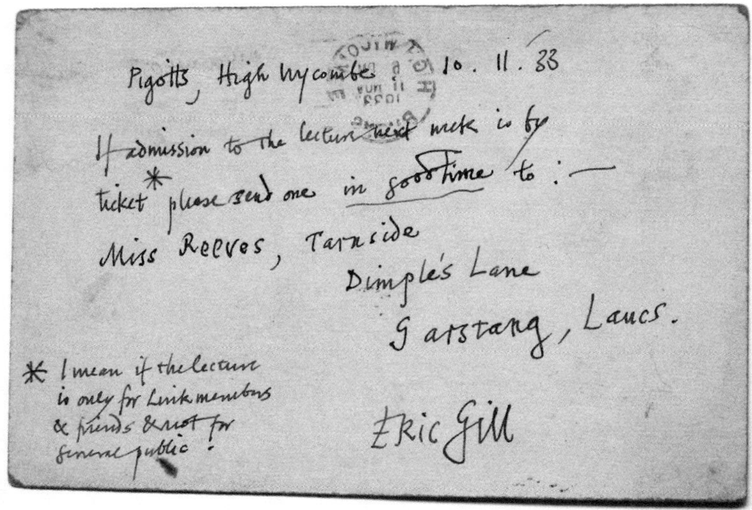

Fig. 21. Postcard sent by Eric Gill requesting a ticket for May Reeves to
attend the Manchester lecture.

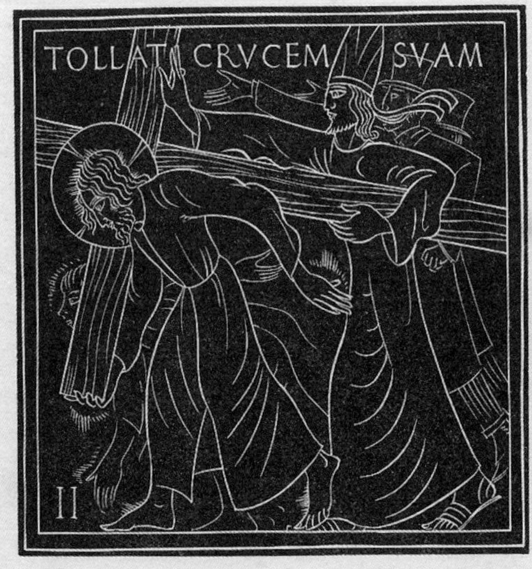

Fig. 22. Front cover of Gill's *Stations of the Cross and Social Justice.*

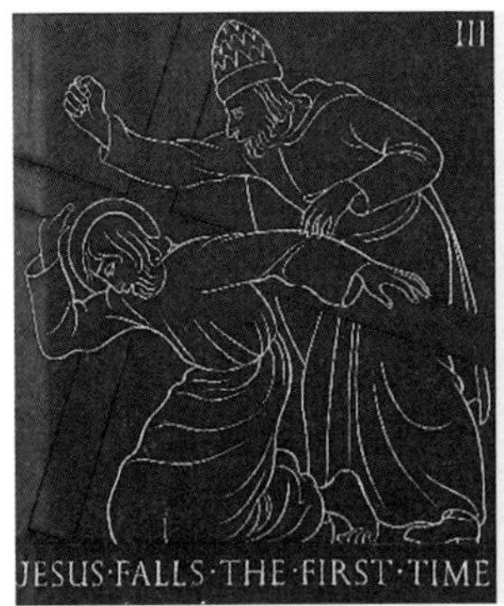

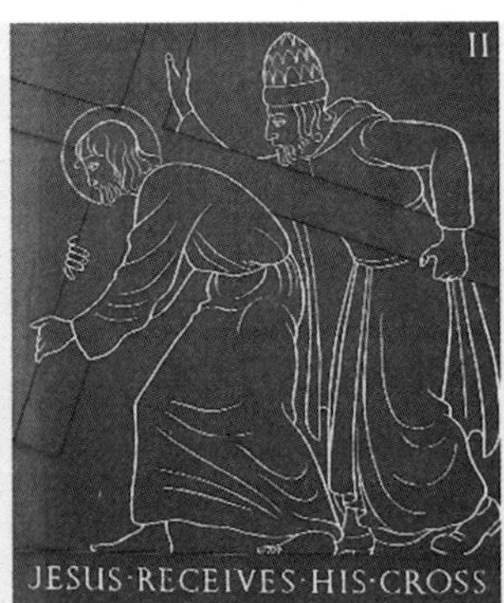

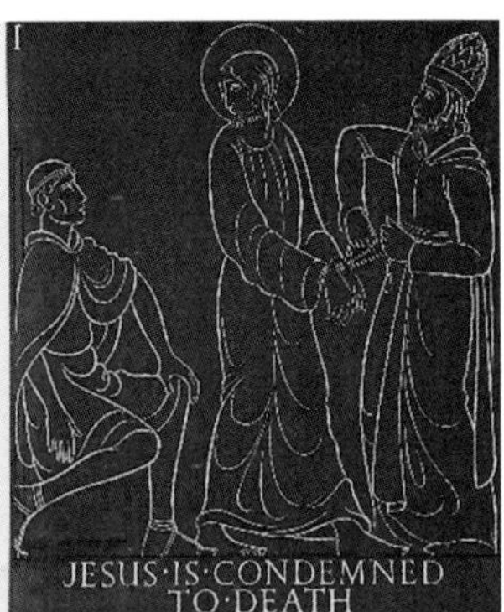

Fig. 23. [right] *First Station of the Cross,* from Gill's carved wood series.
Fig. 24. [center] *Second Station of the Cross,* from Gill's carved wood series.
Fig. 25. [left] *Third Station of the Cross,* from Gill's carved wood series.

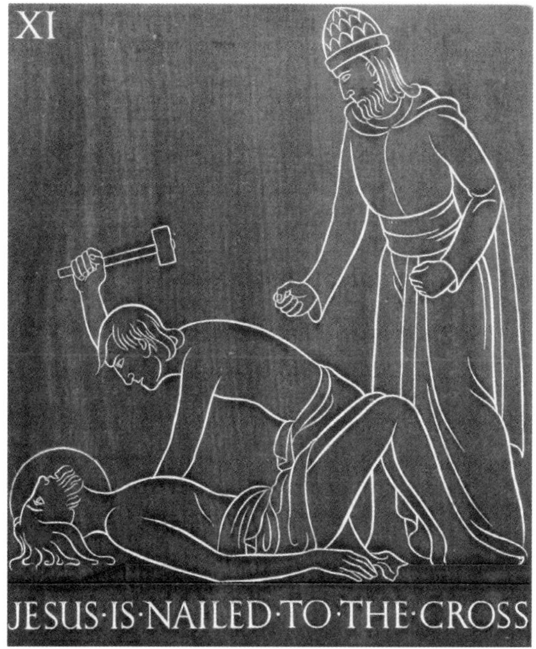

Fig. 26. *Eleventh Station of the Cross*, from Gill's carved wood series.

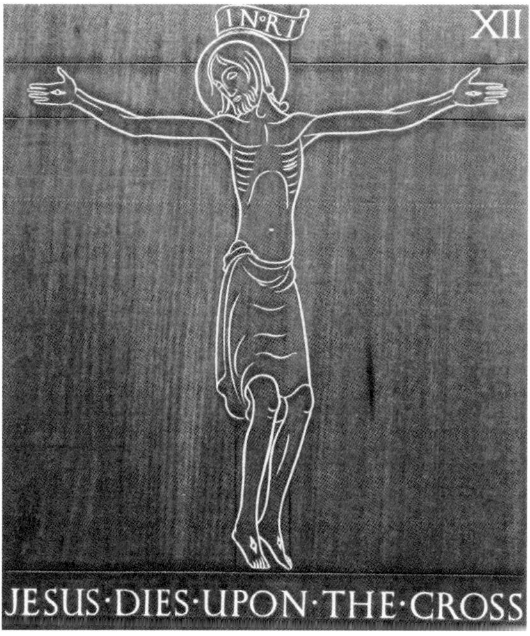

Fig. 27. *Twelfth Station of the Cross*, from Gill's carved wood series.

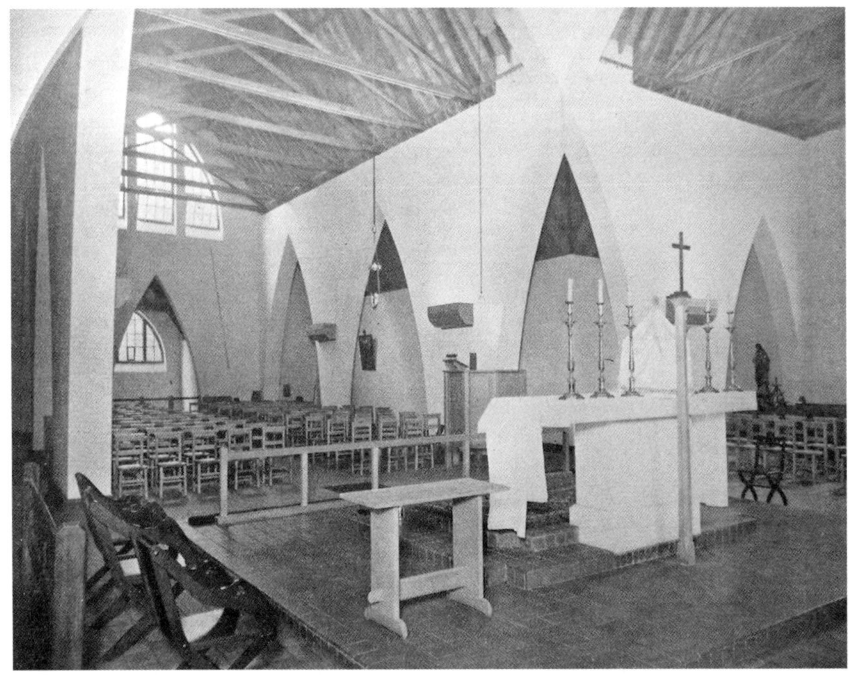

Fig. 28. Interior of St Peter's church, Gorleston.

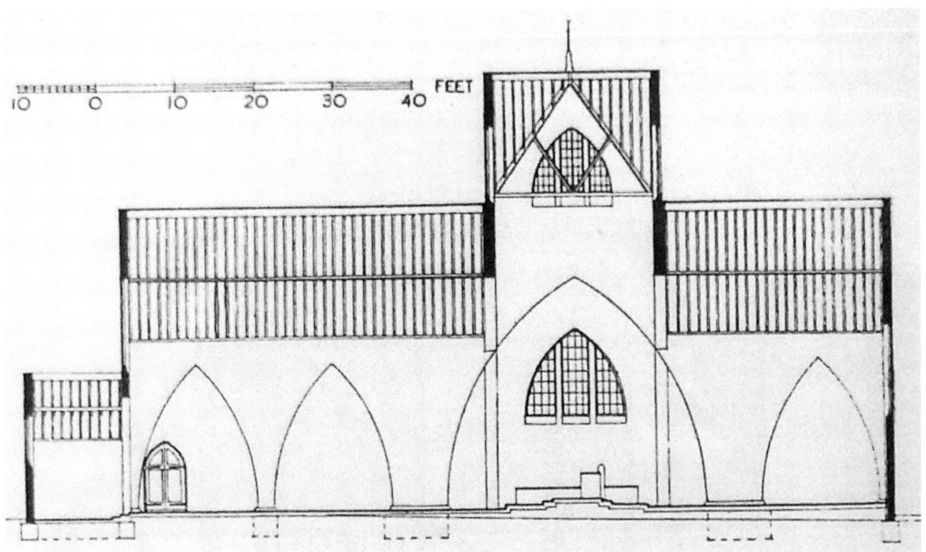

Fig. 29. Side elevation of St Peter's, Gorleston.

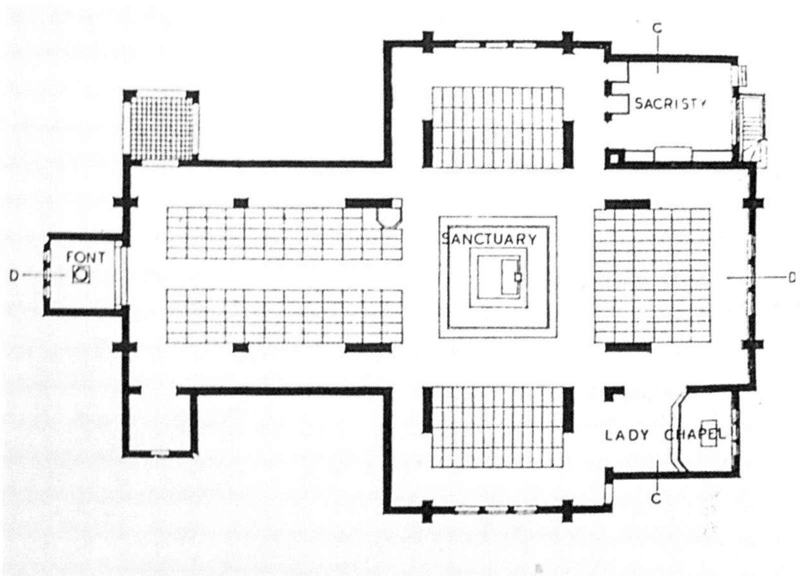

Fig. 30. Plan of St Peter's, Gorleston.

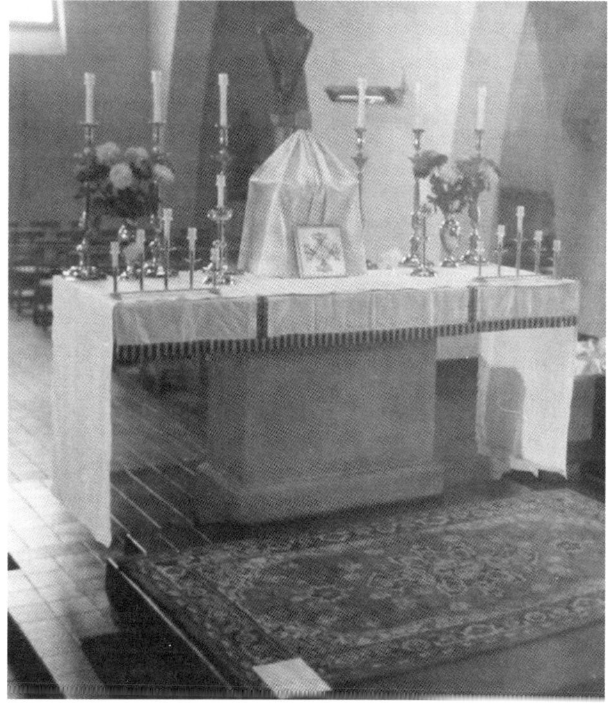

Fig. 31. The altar at St Peter's, Gorleston.

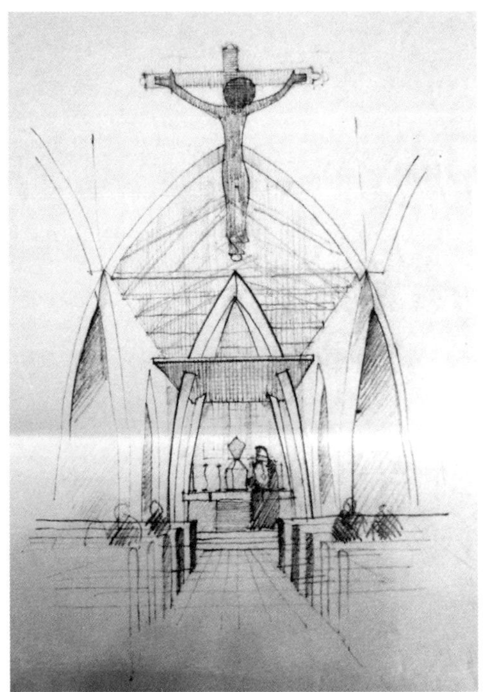

Fig. 32. Proposed baldacchino for St Peter's, Gorleston.

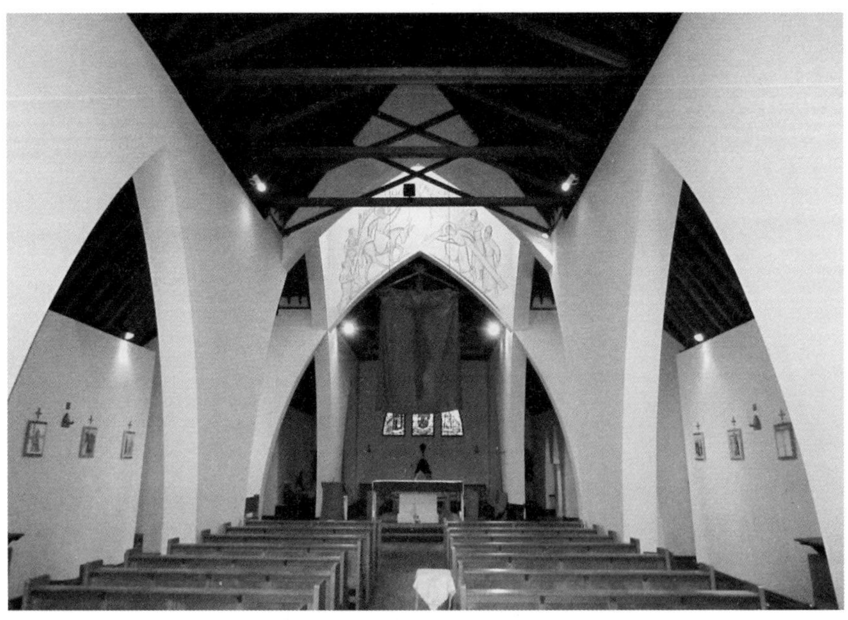

Fig. 33. Interior of St Peter's, Gorleston, Lent 2013.

Chasing the provenance of Eric Gill's wooden Stations of the Cross[*]

Michael Curran FSC

It is well known that Eric Gill produced four distinct sets of the Stations of the Cross carved in stone: Westminster Cathedral (1913–18), St Cuthbert's, Bradford (1921–24), Our Lady & St Peter, Leatherhead, Surrey (1924–25), and St Alban the Martyr, Oxford 1938–1940 (completed after his death). What is generally not known is that he produced a fifth set carved in wood; this chapter traces their provenance.

The story begins many years prior to the creation of these Stations of the Cross, which once adorned the walls of the original St Augustine Catholic church at High Wycombe, Buckinghamshire, and are now owned by the De La Salle Trust. The De La Salle Order was founded over 300 years ago in Rheims by John Baptist De La Salle, in response to the need to educate boys from poor families, so that they could escape out of the poverty into which they were born.

In 1912 the De La Salle Brothers bought a house, 'Castlemount', in Dover, this was to become their Novitiate and Scholasticate. Here the young Brothers received their spiritual formation as well as gaining the necessary teaching qualifications. It was to this house in 1935 that a certain Robert Manley came as a novice. Due to ill health he had to leave, but he kept in contact with the Brothers and I believe that he especially kept in touch with Br David Leo, who took under his wing any novice who was having a difficult time. We will return to Robert Manley and Br David later.

In 1939, only one year before his death, Eric Gill was asked by Fr Lockyer, the parish priest of St Augustine's, High Wycombe, to make a set of Stations of the Cross for his Church. What prompted Fr Lockyer to approach Gill? How could his parish afford them? The Oxford Stations would cost £350 (the approximate price of a three bedroom house in the Home Counties). A clue can be found in

* I am grateful for the assistance of Sheila Mawhood, the archivist of St Augustine's Church, High Wycombe, and for the research carried out on my behalf by Carol Sommer from UCLA. The work presented here would not have been possible without free access to the archives of the De La Salle Brothers.

Fiona MacCarthy's biography of Gill, for she says that in 1938 – the same year that Fr Lockyer came to High Wycombe – a Dr Patrick Flood became the new chaplain at Pigotts, where Gill had lived since 1928; MacCarthy speaks of Flood being partial to a drink and how Fr Lockyer was among his drinking partners.[1]

In August 1938 Fr Lockyer wrote in the parish log-book: 'the church within and without was in a sorry state.' Further on he says that: 'The Bishop was consulted and agreed to the disposal of the existing stations of the X. Eric Gill A.R.A. D.Litt, was asked to design the altar and canopy and new stations. The antependia, tabernacle veils, new purple and white vestments were designed and made at Downside Abbey. A copper collection was taken each Sunday at the doors until the whole cost was paid off.'[2]

It is well known that Gill had high, if not romantic, ideals about not making huge profits from his work – yet he had to make a living and could be very business-like.[3] Gill's account ledgers record that on 1 October 1939 Fr Lockyer paid £10 for the Stations of the Cross.[4] Since no other payments are to be found, one may conclude that £10 was the total cost. From the same page in the ledger one can see that each of the original sycamore panels was bought for 11/- 10^{d} from Cornelissen & Sons, a London art shop still trading today, but with no records relating to this time. Interestingly, the name Denis Tegetmeier, Gill's son-in-law (married to Petra Gill), appears in the debit section. Also, the ledger shows that Fr Lockyer was only asked to pay cost price.

Did Gill carve them himself? Gill preferred to carve in stone; wooden carvings leaving his workshop under his name were drawn by him, but often carved by his assistants. Gill kept meticulous notes in his diaries; for example, he records drawing the design for the fourth Station of the Oxford series on 12 May 1939; on 30 and 31 of May he cut the line and on 1 June he coloured it in. There are no similar entries in his diaries for the wooden Stations, which leads to the possible conclusion that he did not carve them. The only entry relating to these Stations is for the 30 September 1940: 'to H.W. with Denis T[egetmeier]. 11.0 to see Fr. Lockyer re Sta. of †.'[5]

Denis Tegetmeier is once again linked with the wooden Stations; one can reasonably conclude therefore that he was involved in the carving the panels using Gill's drawings. The similarity with the Oxford Stations lends assurance to their having been drawn by Gill himself, this is further supported by the fact

---

1   Fiona MacCarthy, *Eric Gill* (London, 19), p. 288.
2   Archive of St Augustine's RC church, High Wycombe, parish logbook.
3   See above p. 72. n. 96.
4   William Andrews Clark Memorial Library, UCLA, Gill account ledgers.
5   Clark Library, UCLA, Eric Gill Diary, 30 Sept. 1940.

that he used a similar design for the front cover of his book, *Social Justice and the Stations of the Cross*. (Fig. 22).

In 1956 Fr Robert Manley – the same Robert Manley who had been a De La Salle novice in Dover in 1935 – became the curate at St Augustine's. Fr Bainbridge, the parish priest, was planning a new, replacement church and the Gill Stations were considered to be too small. This was very convenient since some of the parishioners did not like them, referring to them as 'Gill's Breadboards'. Fr Bainbridge presumably did not want them; the replacement Stations were very similar in size but more colourful. It is at this point that Br David Leo re-appears in the story. Fr Manley had remained in contact with Br David, and through him learnt that the De La Salle Brothers were in the process of setting up a new chapel at their recently acquired Dogmersfield College, Hampshire; Br David was a member of the community there and involved in setting up the Novitiate and Scholasticate.

A memoir written by Brother David states that Fr Bainbridge was keen for the Brothers to have the Gill Stations of the Cross, and that he only wanted the nominal sum of £100 as payment, even though he was advised that in America he would get £250 for them. However, the 1956 accounts for Dogmersfield show that only £40 was given to Fr Bainbridge. No mention is made of further payments and there is no record in the accounts for St Augustine's church of money being received for the Stations.

Between 1962 and 1964 a new chapel was built at Dogmersfield; the Stations were now in need of renovation. The Brothers were at this time in contact with John Skelton regarding the cutting of a memorial stone for the new chapel. Skelton was a nephew of Gill (the son of his sister Angela) and was the last apprentice he engaged before he died. Skelton, who had a son at the Brothers' school in Brighton, was asked to restore the Stations. The Dogmersfield accounts at the time show that when the new chapel was built, £109.19s.6d was spent on the Stations. When it closed in 1973 the Stations were moved to a newly-built chapel at St Joseph's College, Ipswich, Suffolk. In the mid-nineties, when that College became a separate Trust, the Stations were again removed; this time to a Brothers' Community chapel, where they remain to this day.

A Closer Look at the Wooden Stations (Figs. 28–32)

The panels are 13½ inches wide by 16 inches high. They are made of sycamore wood screwed to a wooden frame and stained brown. The incised lines are coloured in white, gold or black. The inscription (1⅜ inches high) is carved in Gill's own letter-face and coloured white. Each panel is numbered using Roman numerals, again coloured white. In Judith Collins's *Eric Gill: The Sculpture*, these Stations are catalogued as No.299.[6] In the same book a similar carving appears (No.296),[7] commissioned in September 1940 by a Fr Bruno Tausig. It is documented that this carving was drawn by Gill and was largely cut by Tegetmeier; in this instance the wood is not stained, and the incised lines are picked out in black. So, the question arises, were the wooden Stations of the Cross at High Wycombe originally stained or were they stained by Skelton during their restoration? Oral evidence, taken from those who remember them being in the old church at High Wycombe, and also from their time at Dogmersfield before they were renovated, suggests that the wood was of a dark colour and that the lines were coloured black. However, those interviewed were not certain if the panels had actually been stained. There is no conclusive evidence therefore regarding the original colouration of the panels; the question of whether they were originally stained brown or had simply become darkened with age remains unanswered.

The wooden Stations, being designed at the end of Gill's life, reflect his political and spiritual understanding.[8] Politically, Gill was against the exploitation of manual workers by people with power, e.g. financiers. Sometimes he would include in his designs a message aimed at those who were employing him. This was particularly so in the instance of the Leeds war memorial, where he incorporated factory owners, their wives and servants; the Scripture passage he chose for the memorial is that of Christ turning the money-changers out of the temple. The wooden Stations are a further echo of Gill's views regarding social justice. This we can see in the character which appears on the far right-hand side in the first three, and in the eleventh Station (Figs. 23–26). Who is this figure? In the Scriptural accounts of Jesus before Pilate we read how the chief priests, the elders and the scribes were present. The chief priests of that time wore, among other insignia, a white linen robe and a turban, representing the dignity of their office. Gill portrays the figure in the Stations dressed in stylised clothing redolent of the high priests' vestments and wearing what looks like a papal tiara. Compare this to the front cover of *Social Justice and the Stations of the Cross* (Fig. 22); here the religious character is wearing a similar long robe but on his head he has a bishop's mitre.[9] The cover illustration is attributed to Gill. Financiers in top hats

---

6   Judith Collins, *Eric Gill: The Sculpture* (London, 1998), p. 229.

7   *Ibid.*, p. 227.

8   As Naomi Billingsley has noted in her chapter above, Gill's ideas about the subject of the Stations shifted quite radically over a period of time. Cf above, pp. 41–2.

9   Between the earliest forms of the papal tiara and the bishop's mitre there was no difference. With reference to the mitre, *The Catholic Encyclopaedia* notes: 'Whether any influence was exerted by the recollection of the sacerdotal head-ornament of the high-priest of the Old Testament is not known, but probably not – at least there us no trace of any such influence.

are shown standing shoulder to shoulder with the bishop-like figure. A young boy, representing the poor, is alongside Christ, both of whom are being crushed by the weight of the burden placed on their shoulders. The first meditation in *Social Justice and the Way of the Cross* – 'The Condemnation' – speaks of 'The mob inflamed by the religious leaders and politicians and financiers.'[10] By their inclusion in word and image in the Stations Gill is clearly commenting on the role played by the religious leaders in the condemnation and death of Christ. The fact that he portrays them wearing the head attire of contemporary religious leaders is an oblique comment on their role in the modern world. Gill was very critical of the clergy maintaining silence in the face of social injustice. In his opinion, by not condemning injustice they were not properly exercising their authority and so failing to help lift the heavy burden from people's shoulders. The wooden Stations are a pictorial representation of the ideals regarding social justice which he preached – this being the operative word – during his life; many of which can be found in *Chapter Six* above, where his lecture on 'Money and Morals' and its attendant criticism of the clergy is analysed. His strongest criticism during that lecture was that priests, and by implication, bishops, were not making known the teachings of Popes Leo XIII and Pius XI as expressed in the encyclicals *Rerum Novarum* and *Quadragesimo Anno*.

Gill's spiritual understanding can be found throughout the fourteen Stations; for example, the twelfth Station, the Crucifixion (Fig. 27). Here we see Christ as he would appear on an early crucifix: upright, alone, not in pain, not struggling, accepting in faith the will of his Father in Heaven. For the early Christians, the suffering Christ was not a dominant part of their theology. The theology of the Suffering Servant was developed much later, and is dramatically depicted in the sixteenth century Isenheim Altarpiece by Grunewald. Gill was known to frequent the V&A, where he may have looked at the early icons depicting Christ upright and evidently free of pain. A further understanding of this carving can be gained from Gill's 1939 meditations on the Stations of the Cross in which he writes,

> 'The sufferings of Christ *on* the cross are not the chief thing. .. The chief thing *now* to be thought of is that He is lifted up. And "if I be lifted up, I shall draw all men unto me". The standard is raised…He is shown to the world.'[11]

It was not until the mitre was universally worn by bishops that it was called an imitation of the Jewish sacerdotal head-ornament.' *The Catholic Encyclopaedia* (New York, 1913), vol. ix, pp. 404ff.

10 Eric Gill, 'The Stations of the Cross', *Blackfriars*, vol. 18. no. 209. August 1937, pp. 580ff.

11 Eric Gill, *Social Justice & The Stations of the Cross*, (London, 1939), p. 17. For a review see the *Catholic Herald*, 19 May 1939.

In 'Art and Love' Gill speaks of the centrality of the Crucifixion as: 'the image not of the metaphysical fact of universal love but of the physical fact of God's love for man'.[12] This belief he portrayed visually in the Stations, carved in wood and stone, and audibly in *Social Justice and the Stations of the Cross*. Thus in image and word Gill proclaimed what was central to his religion, to his politics and to his spirituality.

12 Quoted in Judith Collins, *op. cit.*, p. 24. This theme is further explored in *Chapter Two* above, especially in reference to Gill's *The Nuptials of God*.

'A Canopy over an Altar': Eric Gill's church of St Peter, Gorleston, Norfolk

Andrew Derrick

The church of St Peter at Gorleston was a late architectural debut for Eric Gill, built towards the end of his life in 1939 (Plate 6). The job was obtained through a network of contacts, which included such notable figures in the interwar English Catholic scene as G.K. Chesterton and Mgr John O'Connor. This essay will focus on the church's liturgical significance rather than its architectural or artistic qualities and will suggest (tentatively) that for all its liturgical innovation, the design is also inspired by an ancient building at the heart of Catholic Christianity.

Early architectural training and influences

Although much better known as a letter-carver and sculptor, Gill trained as an architect. In 1900, at the age of eighteen, he entered the Westminster office of W. D. Caroe, who had a predominantly ecclesiastical (Anglican) practice. Here he found the strict demarcation between gentlemen architects and below-stairs draughtsmen and pupils profoundly dispiriting, such separation offending his emerging notion of the complete artist, 'the integral man'.[1] While at Caroe's office, he met the calligrapher Edward Johnston, whose influence more than any other led Gill away from architecture. Nevertheless, he always valued the disciplines instilled during his time in Caroe's office, 'to such an extent that he clung to the theory that all painters and sculptors, even poets and musicians should receive an architectural training'.[2] As a maker and a workman, Gill drew his artistic (and to some extent his political) ideas from William Morris and Ruskin, and from the artists and architects of the Arts and Crafts movement. He later rejected Chipping Campden Socialism, and distanced himself from the effeminacy, teetotalism, vegetarianism and general affectation he saw in the Arts and Crafts movement. 'I spend all my spare time trying to smash the arts and

---

1 Quoted in Fiona MacCarthy, *Eric Gill* (London, 1989), p. 41.
2 *Ibid.*, p. 39.

crafts "movement" ' he wrote; 'let art take care of itself as it very well can'.[3]

Fiona MacCarthy asks the question 'how modernist *was* Gill?'[4] Her answer was that he was 'too English — and probably too Catholic — for outright modernism'. Despite his troubling erotomania, Gill was a puritan by nature, at least artistically. This was due in part to his Nonconformist upbringing, reinforced by his coming of age in an atmosphere of fierce reaction against the excesses of Victorian taste. Words of highest approbation for Gill were 'good', 'honest' and 'plain'; he abhorred what he described as 'architectooralooralism', and was uninterested, for example, in the sculptural possibilities of reinforced concrete. His puritanism was rooted artistically in the Arts and Crafts movement, and not the rather different puritanism of continental architectural modernism.

Despite its liturgical innovation, the church at Gorleston was conventional in its construction and design. It was built of traditional load-bearing brick, plastered internally, with a timber roof covered with pantiles. Notable influences were two major Arts and Crafts churches built about the time of Gill's architectural apprenticeship: William Lethaby's All Saints, Brockhampton, Herefordshire (1901–2) and E. S. Prior's St Andrew, Roker (1905–7). Both, like Gorleston, have interiors distinguished by great unmodulated arches sweeping up from the floor. None can be described as modernist. The church at Gorleston was built at a time when Gill had established himself as a sculptor, engraver, letter designer and essayist. Public sculptures, notably the figures of Prospero and Ariel on the front of Broadcasting House in London, and the Stations of the Cross in Westminster Cathedral had been widely publicised and generally praised. Gorleston is an unexpected late flowering of Gill's talent, and can be seen as the summation of his life's work and beliefs; 'Gill seized on the project as a long-awaited opportunity to put into practice a multitude of related ideas about building, preaching, singing, church history, world politics, all burgeoning out from the elementary question: What is a church?'[5]

What *is* a church ?

Gill's answer to the question was simple; a church exists 'first and chiefly as a canopy over an altar'.[6] He set forth his ideas in an essay 'Mass for the Masses', which was published in 1938 (the year of his appointment at Gorleston) in *The Cross and the Plough*, a Catholic Distributist periodical. Gill saw contemporary

3   *Ibid.*, pgs. 93 & 94.
4   *Ibid.*, p. 252.
5   *Ibid.*, pp. 279–80.
6   Eric Gill, 'Plain Architecture', *Beauty looks after Herself* (London, 1933), p. 156.

church design in the West as the product of a depraved capitalist system. His solution lay in a reform of worship and liturgy (design would look after itself):

> There is one thing which must be done, and it must be done immediately; for the time is short. But it is a very big thing as well as a very simple one. It is a very revolutionary thing…The altar must be brought back again into the middle of our churches, in the middle of the congregation, surrounded by the people – and the word surrounded must be taken literally. It is essential that the people should be on all sides, in front and behind. The Holy Sacrifice must be offered thus, and in relation to this reform nothing else matters…At the present time it is the custom to place the altar at the end of the church, very often in a specially built apse or chancel and generally separated from the people by the seats of the ministers…There is thus a monstrous division between the place of the altar and the rest of the church. The sanctuary is ruled off as being not merely a holy place but a mysterious place - a place in which only professional feet may tread (priests, clergy, etc.), a place in which the laity can only enter, more or less timidly, when they go up to receive the Communion.[7]

Anticipating the justification that accompanied many liturgical re-orderings after the Second Vatican Council, Gill argued that existing sanctuaries must also be rearranged:

> The choir and the organ, the vestments and the stained glass windows, the carvings, the paintings and the statues, all are so much frippery compared with the altar and the service of the altar. And it is inevitable that such things should be, in literal fact, little better than frippery today. They are not the product of the people's hands. They are for the most part mere merchandise, stuff produced like everything else not for any use, holy or unholy, but for profit. Away with them – if that be too difficult for our feebleness, at least let us disregard them; for merely to remove frippery, to wallow in an orgy of good taste is not itself of any value at all…It will, of course, be said that this suggestion will violate all the architectural arrangements, as well as affront our ancient customs. But architectural and our more or less quaint customs are of no importance compared with the vital necessity of our time. Some will say that the altar will not look nice where we suggest putting it; that is not the question. The only question is where it would be right.[8]

He then sets out his vision of a future, reformed church interior:

> You see … a plain building, and in the apparent centre of it, whatever its actual geometrical shape, slightly raised so that it may be visible to all, the altar with crucifix above or upon it. The people are on all sides, the Mass proceeds, whether

7 *Ibid.*, p. 9.
8 *Ibid.*, pgs 9 & 10.

in Latin or in English or any other language. Everybody can see what is being done…There is no choir or organ business to distract them, no imitation Gothic windows, no frippery of any kind.[9]

In a letter to Fr Walker accompanying his drawings, he argued that the 'mysterious' aspect of religious observance had been over-emphasised, at the expense of the evangelical aspect:

> It is of course actually impossible to exaggerate the mysteriousness, but it is easily possible to under-do the evangelical; and one of the ways in which the loss of contact is most apparent in the tradition which has grown up and placed the altar away from the people at the East end of the church.[10]

In agreeing to a central altar, Fr Walker was assured by Gill that he would be taking part in 'a great movement for the re-evangelisation of the people'.

In supporting more active participation of the laity and a 'demystifying' of the Mass, Gill was embracing ideas which were gaining increasing currency on the Continent in the early decades of the twentieth century, but had as yet made little headway in England. While Gill was clearly aware of these developments, it is not clear whether he knew of their architectural expression in, for example, the centrally-planned churches of Dominikus Böhm, Martin Weber and Rudolph Schwarz. However, he certainly knew about the pioneering church of The First Martyrs, Bradford, built in 1934–5 from designs by Jack Langtry-Langton, and the first centrally-planned Catholic church in England. Gill was commissioned to provide a stone statue of St John Bosco in the narthex, and was aware of the church's liturgical significance (although he was less impressed by its neo-Romanesque architecture).

First Martyrs, its dedication signifying a return to apostolic simplicity, was built by Fr (Monsignor from 1937) John O'Connor. Fr O'Connor had been a close friend of G.K. Chesterton, whom he received into the Catholic faith in 1922, and whose requiem Mass he celebrated at Westminster Cathedral in 1936. He was the model for Chesterton's Fr Brown. He was also a longstanding friend and confidant of Eric Gill, and was associated with the Guild of St Joseph and Dominic, founded by Gill, Hilary Pepler, Desmond Chute and Joseph Cribb at Ditchling in 1921. It was at about that time that Fr O'Connor commissioned Gill to make the Stations of the Cross for St Cuthbert's, Bradford, a chapel-of-ease to First Martyrs.

Before Gorleston, in 1938, Gill had been able to put his liturgical ideas into practice when asked by Dr Neville Gorton, headmaster of Blundell's School at

---

9   *Ibid.,* p. 10.
10 Quoted in MacCarthy, *op. cit.,* p. 280.

Tiverton, to re-design and simplify the Tractarian chancel of the school chapel. Gill placed a new stone altar at its centre, carved and painted by the boys under his supervision. Five years later, Dr Gorton was appointed Bishop of Coventry where, citing the influence of Gill, he commissioned Giles Gilbert Scott to produce a design for the rebuilding of the bombed-out cathedral, with a free-standing altar under a baldacchino (Scott's scheme was abandoned after criticism from the Royal Fine Art Commission).[11] Meanwhile, Gill's altar at Blundell's was removed as soon as Gorton left for Coventry, ending up 'in a home for unmarried mothers';[12] happily it has since been returned.

Church of St Peter, Gorleston

It appears that Gill obtained the commission to build the church and presbytery at Gorleston through the influence of his friend and High Wycombe neighbour Joseph Edward ('Eddie') Nuttgens.[13] The stained glass artist was a friend of Fr Thomas Walker, who as priest at High Wycombe had prepared Chesterton (who lived nearby at Beaconsfield) for First Communion and Confirmation after the writer's conversion in 1922.[14]

In 1928 Fr Walker was transferred to Gorleston, on the east coast near Great Yarmouth (both parishes being then in the Diocese of Northampton). The local Catholic congregation had outgrown the converted malthouse in which it had worshipped since 1889, and wished to build a new church on a site which had been acquired about twenty five years earlier (largely from a local grocer's legacy). To offset any concerns about his qualifications for the job, Gill reassured Mgr Youens, Bishop of Northampton, that he had experience as 'a working builder', referring probably to the modest chapel he had designed and had built at Ditchling Common. However, he was also prudent enough to enlist the help of Edmund Farrell, a High Wycombe architect. The builders were H. R. Middleton & Co. of Great Yarmouth. The foundation stone was laid by Bishop Youens on 28 February 1939; building work was rapid, and the completed church was opened by Bishop Youens on 14 June in the same year. The final cost came in under the contract price of £6,775.

A description of the church interior (Fig. 28), plan and section (Figs. 29 and 30), probably written by Gill (or by Farrell under Gill's influence), was published in *The Architect and Building News* on 8 December 1939:

11   See Thomas, J., *Coventry Cathedral* (New Bell's Cathedral Guides, Unwin Hyman, 1987), pp. 82–6.

12   Robert Speaight, *Life of Eric Gill* (London, 1966), p. 261.

13   *Ibid.*, 279.

14   Ian Ker, *G. K. Chesterton: A Biography* (Oxford, 2011), p. 690.

> The controlling factor in the design of this church was the centrally placed altar. The seating for the congregation of about 100 is planned on four sides of the altar so that all may see the ceremony and take an intimate part in the service. The plan provides an open central space, not impeded by piers, and cruciform space for the congregation. In the south-east angle a Lady Chapel is provided and a sacristy and confessionals are planned in the north-east angle [...] Pointed arches were asked for by the client. This provided the opportunity for building in a strictly functional manner with brick. The main structural feature of interest is the crossing of the central arches, which provides an octagonal central space lighted from windows in the four sides of the small tower above. To avoid the expense of pillars the arches spring from floor level: the lines connecting the bases, and the apex, forming an equilateral triangle. The height from floor to apex is approximately 18ft. Over the altar is a large hanging crucifix designed by Eric Gill and executed by Donald Potter. On the east wall of the tower there is a painting by Denis Tegetmeier and on the north porch wall a carving of St Peter executed by Anthony Foster. Both were designed by Eric Gill. Internal and external finishes are simple. Internal walls are plastered and the floor is tiled. The windows are glazed with clear glass. Artificial lighting is from wall brackets.

Gill was pleased with the church, with reservations. On 20 June 1939 he wrote to Fr Desmond Chute:

> I hope you will get to Norwich and therefore to Gorleston. G. is about three miles along the coast south of Great Yarmouth. Anyone will tell you where the new Catholic church is – it is pretty conspicuous and as it was opened last Wednesday with a great flourish, the whole town is aware of its existence. I very much hope you will like this building, although there are many things we would do differently next time – for instance, the east, south, and north windows are too big and too low and the panes of glass too big; the red-tiled steps of the Altars are not satisfactory, the little Crucifix over the main Altar is not really a Christian work though it says the right word, I think; the Crucifix (Anthony F's) over the Lady Chapel Altar is a failure and will be replaced by another. I hope you like Denis' paintings and the big Crucifix, also Anthony Foster's carvings on the porch, and I hope you will like the big crossed arches.[15]

The significance of the church was recognised by *The Catholic Herald*, in its report of the opening ('a departure which may have a great bearing on the modern liturgical movement')[16] and in a review by the writer and critic Joan Morris.[17] While generally favourable, Morris's review was not uncritical:

15   Walter Shewring (ed.), *Letters of Eric Gill* (London, 1947), p. 419.
16   *Catholic Herald*, 23 June 1939.
17   *Catholic Herald*, 1 Sept. 1939.

The new Catholic Church at Gorleston-on-Sea, Norfolk, designed by Eric Gill, is an event in the history of English architecture. It is undoubtedly truly English; there is no trace of Italian or French, and although there are some points of resemblance to the German church at Neu-Ulm,[18] in which the same form of arches are used, yet the different plan and material used make it essentially characteristic of England. [...] Passing from the oppression of the totally red exterior, one enters into a startling entirely white interior, with pointed arches rising straight from the ground. The extreme change creates an impression of relief and joy, uplifting one spiritually.

The altar is placed in the middle of the four transepts of the Greek cross, permitting the people to see the altar from all sides. The altar consists of a long slab of stone placed on a shorter slab. The floor and three steps of the altar are in red tiles. Had Gill kept consistently to his theory of the 'useful' he would not have made the altar so low. When alone in the church the proportions appear perfect, but it is rather aggravating when others come in and sit right in front of you, blocking all the view. For practical purposes a higher altar would be more convenient.

Though the idea of a central altar is interesting and is being tried in several other places, there are nevertheless a number of drawbacks. Present-day rubrics insist on having the Tabernacle on the altar with a crucifix, and a suitable throne for the Exposition of the Blessed Sacrament is required. In a large church or cathedral a special chapel or altar can be set aside for this, but in a medium-sized church, as at Gorleston, this is an impossible luxury. With all these things, therefore, on the altar, there is a definite back and front to it, and the people at the back cannot enjoy Mass very well, with the effect that they all crowd into the front. [...]

The electric light has most unfortunately been enclosed in very heavy wooden cases attached to the wall; they look like supports to carry large statues. With all the new inventions as to means of lighting it seems incredible that something neater could not have been thought out.

Gill did not let these comments pass, and was particularly sensitive to any criticism of the altar. He was however ready to apologise for the electric light boxes; as can be seen from a letter to Graham Carey, he had installed lighting and heating only reluctantly.[19] As the country was going to war, Gill replied:

18   Presumably Dominikus Böhm's church of St John the Baptist, Neu-Ulm (1922). That church was notable as an experiment in the sculptural use of reinforced concrete. The writer was correct in seeing Gill's church as thoroughly English.

19   'It's free, I think, from architectooralooralism [sic] and it's free, apart from electric lighting (which I can't refuse to install) & heating (which, again, I can't resist – tho. I think it's a shocking waste of money), apart from these it's free from industrial products.' See *Letters of Eric Gill*, p. 414.

From our point of view the success of the building is that, being, by the good will and perspicacity of the Bishop and his advisers, allowed to build a church with a central altar, we have succeeded in solving the problem of getting a big central space by crossing the arches and without recourse to anything but plain bricklayers' and carpenters' work. That is the point – the whole point. It is not that the idea of a central altar is 'interesting'. The point is that it is apostolic; it is a move in the direction implied by Catholic Action. Your readers are misled if they are led to suppose that the thing was done for the looks of it. For the same reason we avoided the medievalism of leaded glass. Why should there be a divorce of domestic from church building? […]

I agree that the altar is too low, but not that the presence of the tabernacle upon it seriously impedes the assistance of those who are placed facing the priest. Your critic says they 'cannot enjoy Mass very well'. Good Lord! Nothing is more truly enjoyable than Holy Mass, but that's not the reason for our attendance – it's not a Queen's Hall concert or a picture show. The real trouble is not the tabernacle but the loading of the altar with flowers and vases and enormous brass candlesticks. […]

I am sorry about the electric light boxes. But in my view the electric light is entirely unnecessary, for, as Mgr. John O'Connor says: 'You don't go to church to read books'. But as they insisted on electric light we put it in those boxes so that it shouldn't glare in people's eyes.[20]

On the question of obstructed views, they were both right. The bulk of the tabernacle and the loading of the altar with flowers, vases and candlesticks combined to limit visibility from the seating in the eastern arm of the church, as the photograph demonstrates (Fig. 31). Morris's reply to Gill however flushed out her real concern about the central altar – its rejection of rich layers of tradition in the possibly spurious pursuit of 'authenticity':

When I speak about the idea of a central altar as being 'interesting', I mean, of course, from the point of view of a liturgical development, not just an aesthetic experiment in a ground plan. I am, nevertheless, a little suspicious of the 'liturgical revivalists' who wish to return to 'apostolic' customs. You cannot ask the full-blown rose to re-enter its green calix, nor can you expect the Church to limit itself to the liturgical ceremonies of apostolic times. The Apostles themselves would have rejoiced at the present-day devotion in the Exposition of the Blessed Sacrament, which was impossible in their day. […]

We do not attend Mass only to enjoy it. Nevertheless a full view of the ceremonies at the altar is a legitimate desire in order to foster devotion and spiritual enjoyment. My main interest in a central altar is the hope that more people may obtain this view – rather than because it was practised in the times of the Apostles – nevertheless, as I pointed out in my article, there are some difficulties to get over. […]

20 *Catholic Herald*, 8 Sept. 1939.

Eric Gill admits to having left out the electric lights because he does not like people to read books when in church. Though this may be a higher form of prayer, the Church has consideration for all types of people and in all stages of spiritual development. It is hardly fair for an architect to impose his own form of spirituality on a whole parish.[21]

On the question of 'apostolic customs', Gill offered this clarification: 'It may be desirable to point out that when I said that certain things in this church were 'apostolic' I did not use the word in the archeological sense preferred by your critic, but as describing that which bears witness or testimony.'[22]

A Roman precedent?

Gill had travelled twice to Rome, in 1906 and 1925. He attended Mass at St Peter's, a building he disliked, although he admired its architectural form. In 1931 he wrote:

> If some future Pope would have the courage and the power to carve off all the carvings in the Vatican Basilica and remove all the mosaics and paintings, we should have a building so stupendously beautiful that even the lilies of the field … would agree that art improves on nature …[23]

Gill the Puritan had similarly advised Archbishop Hinsley to abandon the programme of mosaic work at Westminster Cathedral in favour of 'whitewash for the walls and domes, thus preserving the very great beauty of the building, as such, and giving light'.[24]

Perhaps the church at Gorleston can be regarded as a scaled down and purified version of St Peter's basilica. The buildings have a common dedication, and what could be more 'apostolic' than to draw inspiration from the church built over the bones of the Prince of the Apostles? St Peter's in Rome is in effect a Greek cross on plan, with one arm (the nave) lengthened, and the altar and tomb of the Apostle placed centrally under the crossing. St Peter's in Gorleston is similar on plan, the sanctuary dais occupying the space of the tomb and, as originally placed, the high altar that of Bernini's high altar and baldacchino. It will not have escaped Gill's notice that the presence of the *confessio* in front of the high altar at the Roman basilica meant that the priest here said Mass *versus populum*. While this was not yet possible at Gorleston, Gill may have wished and planned for such an eventuality. A conscious debt to St Peter's in Rome is not

---

21   *CH*, 15 Sept. 1939.
22   *CH*, 29 Sept. 1939.
23   From Gill's essay, *Clothes* (1931), quoted in Speaight, *op. cit.*, p. 177.
24   Quoted in Speaight, *op. cit.*, p. 284.

recorded in Gill's correspondence or diaries, but the comparisons are intriguing and worthy of further study.

Later alterations

It might be thought that a church so liturgically prescient might more than most have escaped major reordering. This is not so; many changes have been made. On the positive side, the derided electric light boxes are no more. Less welcome has been the replacement of the chairs with benches,[25] the glazing in of the porch (congregations *will* insist on being warm), the removal of Gill's nave pulpit[26] and altar rails, and the poster-colour over-painting of Denis Tegetmeier's Stations of the Cross (which had been introduced in 1962).[27] More debatable has been the introduction of stained glass. Gill would certainly have disapproved, but one window at least, that at the east end (installed in 1963), is a fine piece – ironically enough by Gill's friend Joseph Nuttgens.

Gill's design made no provision for a canopy over the altar, reflecting his view that the church itself was the canopy. Clearly this cut no ice with the bishop, and various plans for a canopy or baldacchino were put forward by Wearing Hastings and Norton of Norwich (Fig. 32). A baldacchino would have only strengthened comparisons with St Peter's basilica, but in the event a simple suspended canopy was installed in 1963, interposed between the altar and Gill's crucifix (which had to be raised).

After the Second Vatican Council, the tabernacle was relocated to the east end of the church. The tiled dais in the sanctuary was remodelled, allowing for the altar to be slightly raised and moved forward so as to be placed centrally under the crossing. However, it was not until the 1990s that the suspended altar canopy was removed and the intended relationship between altar and crucifix restored.

Thus today (Fig. 33), with the major criticisms of the original design overcome, it might be said that Gill's liturgical vision has been fully realised. However, even as adapted for post-Conciliar worship, a problem remains: the eastern arm of the church, intended by Gill for congregational seating, still has its view obstructed - not by the tabernacle, but now by the back of the priest. Perhaps Gill underestimated the practical drawbacks of the centralised plan.

25 Some of the chairs survive, mainly in the Lady Chapel.

26 It survives in part, deposited in the north transept.

27 Similarly inappropriate over-painting of the wall paintings and crucifix over the sanctuary, which had been carried out by a local fairground artist, was removed by the conservator Andrea Kirkham of Norwich in the 1990s, with English Heritage grant aid. The restored paintings can be seen in figure 33.

Select Bibliography

Attwater, Donald, *Modern Christian Revolutionaries* (New York, 1947).

Bagniewski, Melissa, and others, eds, *Posters Held Within the Eric Gill Collection University of Notre Dame* (Notre Dame, 2012).

Browne, John, and Dean, Timothy, *Westminster Cathedral: Building of Faith* (London, 1995).

Collins, Judith, *Eric Gill the Sculpture* (London, 1998).

Cribb, Ruth, and Cribb, Joe, *Eric Gill, Lust for Letter and Line* (London, 2011).

Gaine OP, Simon Francis, *Obituary Notices of the English Dominicans from 1952 to 1966* (Oxford, 2000).

Gill, Eric, *Engravings by Eric Gill: A Selection of Engravings on Wood and Metal representative of his work to the end of the year 1927 with a complete Chronological List of Engravings and a Preface by the Artist* (Bristol, 1929).

Gill, Eric, *Unemployment* (London, 1933).

Gill, Eric, 'Plain Architecture', in *Beauty looks after Herself* (London, 1933).

Gill, Eric, *Money and Morals* (London, 1934).

Gill, Eric, *Social Justice & The Stations of the Cross* (London, 1939).

Gill, Eric, *Autobiography* (London, 1944).

Gill, Eric, *An Essay on Typography*, Christopher Skelton ed., (2nd edn, London, 1988).

Gill, Eric, *Servile Labour and Contemplation* (The Aylesford Press, 1989).

Gill, Evan R., *The Inscriptional Work of Eric Gill* (London, 1964).

Gill, Evan, *A Bibliography*, rev. D. Steven Corey and Julia Mackenzie (2nd edn, Winchester, 1991).

Heppenstall, Rayner, *Four Absentees* (London, 1960).

Hoare, Lottie, *Philip Hagreen: A Sceptic and a Craftsman* <http://www3.nd.edu/~jsherman/hagreen/Hagreen>

Jones, Michael, *Degenerate Moderns* (Ignatius Press, 1993).

Kindersley, David, *Mr Eric Gill Recollections of David Kindersley* (Ward Ritchie Press, 1967).

Lothian, James R., *The Making and Unmaking of the English Catholic Intellectual Community, 1910–1950* (Notre Dame, 2009).

MacCarthy, Fiona, *Eric Gill* (London, 1989).

McCann, Timothy J., ed., *The Eric Gill Collection at Chichester. A Catalogue* (1982).

Maritain, Jacques, *Art and Scholasticism with Other Essays*, trans. J. F. Scanlan (London, 1946).

Mulvey OP, Kieran, *Hugh Pope of the Order of Preachers* (London, 1953).

Peace, David, *Eric Gill The Inscriptions* (London, 1994).

Pepler, Hilary, *The Hand Press* (St Dominic's Press, 1934).

Pepler, Hilary, 'Hampshire House Workshop', *Blackfriars*, 31:359, (Feb.1950).

Pepler, Hilary, *Memorandum*, (St Dominic's Press, n.d.).

Rogers, Patrick, *The Beauty of Stone: The Westminster Cathedral Marble* (London, 2008).

Rogers, Patrick, *Reflections: The Westminster Cathedral Mosaics* (London, 2010).

Rogers, Patrick, *Westminster Cathedral: An Illustrated History* (London, 2012).

Rothenstein, John, *Eric Gill* (London, 1927).

Rowton, E., 'The Stations of the Cross in the Cathedral', *Westminster Cathedral Chronicle*, 12, (March 1918).

Shewring, Walter, ed., *Letters of Eric Gill* (London, 1947).

Skelton, John, 'Eric Gill and Chichester', in Walter Hussey ed., *Chichester 900* (1975).

Speaight, Robert, *The Life of Eric Gill* (London, 1966).

Yorke, Malcolm, *Eric Gill Man of Flesh and Spirit* (London, 1981).